PUNK IS A FOUR-LETTER WORD

by
Ben Weasel

©1991, 1992, 1993, 1994, 1995, 1997, 1998, 1999, 2001 and 2002 by Ben Foster

All rights reserved.

No part of this book may be used or reproduced in any manner whatsoever without written permission except in the case of brief quotations embodied in critical articles and reviews.

Photography by Tim Carlson
Cover Design by John Pierson

Hope And Nonthings
www.hopeandnonthings.com

Printed in the United States Of America
First printing: March 2002

First edition

ISBN # 0-9707458-6-9,
Library Of Congress Control Number:2002104106

Contents

Introduction	1
Maximum Touring	5
Maximum Music	9
Maximum Extra	14
Maximum Liars	18
Maximum Punk & Profit Margins	24
Maximum Isms	30
The Nanny And The Rock Star	34
Maximum Style	50
Punk Is A Four-Letter Word	54
Maximum Style Revisited	58
You Damn Kids With Your Internet And Your Loud Rock Music!	61
Eulogy For A Friend	67
The Runaway	72
The Paper Boy	84
The Janitor	92
The Pizza Boy	98
The Library Aide	104
We Stand On Guard From Thee	116
The New Punk Order	123
Clown For Hire	130
Good Doggy	134
Crimpshrine	137
Practice Does Not Make Perfect	140
The Infinite Joys Of Being A Professional Musician	149

Acknowledgements

The material in this book, except "The Introduction," "The Pizza Boy," and "The Infinite Joys Of Being A Professional Musician," has been previously published in a slightly different form:

"Maximum Touring," *MaximumRockNRoll*, October, 1991
"Maximum Music," *MaximumRockNRoll*, September, 1992
"Maximum Extra," *MaximumRockNRoll*, October, 1992
"Maximum Liars," *MaximumRockNRoll*, March, 1993
"Maximum Punk And Profit Margins," *MaximumRockNRoll*, June, 1994
"Maximum Isms," *MaximumRockNRoll*, November, 1994
"The Nanny And The Rock Star," *Panic Button*, September, 1994
"Maximum Style," *MaximumRockNRoll*, March, 1995
"Punk Is A Four-Letter Word," screechingweasel.com, June, 1997
"Maximum Style Revisited," screechingweasel.com, July, 1997
"You Damn Kids With Your Internet And Your Loud Rock Music!," screechingweasel.com, August, 1997
"Eulogy For A Friend," screechingweasel.com, April, 1998
"The Runaway," *Scam*, 1991
"The Paper Boy," *Panic Button*, June, 1993
"The Janitor," *Panic Button*, September, 1994
"The Library Aide," *Panic Button*, December, 1994
"We Stand On Guard From Thee," *Blood On The Ice*, January, 1997
"The New Punk Order," *10 Things Jesus Wants You To Know*, Fall, 1998
"Clown For Hire," *Hit List*, February/March, 1999
"Good Doggy," *Hit List*, April/May, 1999
"Crimpshrine," Lookout Records catalog, 1998
"Practice Does Not Make Perfect," *Cool Beans*, January, 2001

Thanks to: Dave Awl, Sara Corrigan, Ramsey Kanaan, Steven Malk + John Pierson for suggestions, support, proofing and editing. Special Thanks to: All the Fanzine Editors who have published my writing and especially those who continue to.

for Pixie

INTRODUCTION

I started putting this book together in 1996 with the idea of writing new material that would comprise almost a half of the book. I'm glad I didn't. For one thing, I have a better sense now of what should be included here and what is better left in the slowly decomposing piles of old fanzines laying around in closets and boxes under beds around the world. But I also kept writing for fanzines, and occasionally for a website dedicated to my band, Screeching Weasel. My writing was much better in 1996 than it was when I started in 1987; it's miles better in 2002. That new material was written not under the pressure of filling pages in a book, but out of the need to say something; the same need that got me started on this writing thing in the first place.

In 1987, at age 19, I wrote an accusatory letter to a local fanzine concerning the lack of quality in their record reviews; they seemed to look down on punk rock. They wrote me back and told me that if I thought I could do better I was welcome to join the reviewing staff. That's just sort of the way things used to work in the fanzine world. People did goofy shit like take on some crank to write record reviews just because he insulted them in a somewhat effective manner.

The first incarnation of my record-reviewing career was short-lived. The truth was, I couldn't do better. I hadn't paid much attention on the rare occasions when I'd bothered to attend school so I didn't have much going for me from a technical standpoint. I also knew nothing about developing a voice. I used stupid, inappropriate and often nonsensical similes to describe records. I didn't understand music well enough yet to convey with any intelligence the pros and cons of a given record. I didn't last very long.

But soon enough, I was reviewing records for Jim Testa's *Jersey Beat*. Jim was one of the first prominent fanzine publishers to take an interest in my band and he was the first – by far – to suggest that I might have some writing talent. I'd written a letter to *MaximumRockNRoll* – the biggest and most influential punk fanzine at the time – concerning what I saw as a trend of some of the more popular bands of the day like Sonic Youth and Husker Du regressing into 70's self-indulgence. Sonic Youth went on to reprint it on the insert of one of their records in the shape of a crucifix (what wits!) but at that point I was still not widely known as "that fucking asshole." I earned that jacket – in conjunction with the crowd baiting in which I engaged while my band was on stage – while I was writing for *Jersey Beat*. I was assigned to review the majority of the meat-headed tough guy and straight-edge records coming out of New York and New England. I believe Testa gave me this gig not only because he knew I despised the chest-beating, knuckle-dragging, mouth-breathing idiocy of these glassy-eyed missing links and would thus be prone to tear their records apart in print with an unparalleled gusto, but also because most of the *Jersey Beat* reviewers, unlike me, actually lived and regularly attended shows in the greater New York metropolitan area and were likely to end up on the receiving end of a five-on-one beating should they have the temerity to take a printed piss on the latest Youth Of Today record. Living in Chicago and being a strong believer in carrying Mace, knowing all exits of clubs and using my fast legs to run like crazy if approached by a menacing Neanderthal, I had no qualms about shitting on the tough guys' parade.

After producing an ill-fated, two sided sort of newsletter called "The Slam Sheet" that I used to pass out at shows (often watching as people crumpled or ripped them up just after taking them), I took on the task of doing the Chicago scene reports for *MaximumRockNRoll*. At the time, the scene reports were an important part of MRR. This was before widespread use of fax machines, e-mail and cell phones; for many people, their monthly dose of scene reports in MRR let them know where to try to book their bands on upcoming tours, what the great new bands were in other towns, where to see gigs, get a cheap meal, or find a diner that wouldn't kick you out for nursing the same cup of coffee for six hours straight. All of this didn't make writing (or reading) the scene reports any less boring. In 1990, I tired of doing the scene reports and mentioned to my friend Kamala that I was going to quit because I'd rather be writing a column. Kamala had

MRR head honcho Tim Yohannan's ear and days later he called me to offer me a gig writing a column every other month. They just didn't have space to run my nonsense every issue. After my first column was printed and MRR was flooded with hate mail, Tim called to tell me that I was welcome to write a monthly column if I liked. I did so for another five years.

That was my first real writing. I wrote about what I felt like writing about. I was aggressive, opinionated, judgmental, sarcastic and sometimes downright mean. Learning to write in public is not a good idea. I would think in most cases it would be ugly at best; in my case it was brutal. I haven't included most of the early columns in this collection (in fact, I think there are less than ten in total included here; I wrote more than fifty) for several reasons. Primary among them is the cold, hard fact that they are so poorly written that no amount of editing could save them. I've included some poorly written columns in this collection, but the real stink bombs have been left out. This is not only to save you the trauma of having to read that garbage; my own vanity plays a role in this decision. Another reason is that many of the older columns were mean-spirited and unfair. They attacked individuals, some of whom deserved it and others who didn't, but none who deserved the over-the-top crapola I was happily spewing out of my typewriter at the time.

More than my on-stage antics, my MRR columns developed a rather unsavory reputation for me, which for some insane reason I chose to savor. This helped get both myself and my band some attention but the novelty quickly wore off; it was negative attention, often in the form of some drunken goon wanting to punch my lights out while I was trying to stand on a stage to play my guitar and sing my stupid punk songs. I started lightening up – for the most part – and what I think are the best of those post-dogshit columns are included here.

Also included are pieces I wrote for various fanzines – including my own – over the past eleven years. Some pieces are included simply because they're fairly well-known to fans of my writing who would feel cheated if they were omitted; others are included just because I really like them.

Somewhere along the line, I began to get better as a writer. The pieces in this collection are in more or less chronological order and I can see the quality of my writing improve in a corresponding fashion. I hope you agree. I still have many weaknesses, not the least of which is my tendency to misuse words, often with such authority that only an editor would notice my seemingly flagrant errors. My understanding of basic grammar has improved but my knowledge of punctuation and sentence structure remains limited at best. But I look at writing the same way I've always looked at playing punk rock songs: I have something to say so I'm just going to say it and I won't be stopped by lack of skill. Skill can come later. In many ways it already has but in most ways I'm still miles from mastering the art of writing. That's okay. Most of the pieces in this collection are at least passable, and a few of them are good. In most cases I had a lot of fun writing this stuff. I hope you get some enjoyment out of reading it.

Ben Weasel
2.7.02

MAXIMUM TOURING

Well, I was supposed to keep a tour diary for a certain fanzine but I just never really felt like it so I guess the best I can do is to clue you in to somewhat interesting tour happenings.

MINNEAPOLIS: Nothing interesting happened.

SIOUX FALLS, SD: Three kids came up to me before the show to chat. When they discovered I'm 23 years old, they almost passed out. According to them, 21 is over the hill. I wonder what they'll do with the precious five years they have left. Sioux Falls is the home of a disgusting little establishment called Gigglebees. My band ventured there for dinner with Larry Livermore. It's kinda one of those Showbiz pizza places; lotsa video games and what have you. It also has a mechanical animal — either a rat or a coyote, depending on your view — that rides a bicycle around a train track serving your food and making stupid jokes. I got tired of the fucking thing so I told it to go away. It spent the next twenty minutes hassling me while I tried to consume the gummy pizza. When I got back to the club, several people informed me that the rat had been beheaded several times by angry patrons. I don't blame them.

RAPID CITY, SD: The name is rather misleading. Upon arriving in town, we attempted to find Mt. Rushmore. Every matchbook, billboard, bus stop bench and toilet seat in the state has an advertisement for it but we could not find the fucking thing. We played at some sort of fairgrounds on a stage that doubled as a kitchen. Stayed at a straight-edge house with cool straight guys. Never saw our famous president's faces carved in rock.

BILLINGS, MT: The second scariest town I've ever set foot in. Paint me black and stick me in a Louisiana swamp before you ever send me back there again. Half the people who showed up at the gig sported Doors and Led-Zeppelin t-shirts. Got a break and stayed at a girl's mom's house. Very clean, very quiet and very pleasant. But I was still glad to leave redneck central behind until we reached the scariest town I've ever set foot in:

MISSOULA, MT: The show was wonderful. The people who set up the show were wonderful. Some of the people who came to the show were wonderful. Everybody else was a complete asshole. Standing outside the club, I saw two jock-type fellows walk out the door. As they walked past me, one of them stared me up and down a few times. Curious, I asked "WHAT?" The guy sez, "I was looking at your clothes." His buddy sez, "What the fuck are you saying WHAT to my friend for?" I say, "Cause he was looking at my clothes." Then he starts the usual schoolyard shit about, hey are you looking for a fight? I told him I thought HE was looking for a fight. He asked me if I wanted to start shit. I told him NO. They walked slowly to their car with the license plates that read BOZE MAN. They stared me down for a few minutes and left. I took a walk around the block and then slipped back into the club for a few minutes. A mad mosher slammed into my bass player who was standing at the edge of the crowd. Dave gently nudged the guy away. He crouched down and started screaming, "Come on, motherfucker!" I went back outside. Huey and Louie the punx were there. Huey asked me if I was just in the club. I told him yes.

"Where?" asks Huey.

"All around." I'm getting impatient with this goof.

"Well," barks Huey, "you look like the guy who stole my friend's wallet."

Oh I do, do I? I've had it with this shit. My frustrations start pouring out and Huey looks confused. He puts his hands up and sez, "No, man, I just thought you kinda looked like the guy, that's all."

We agonize for a while after the gig and finally decide to cut out to the next town that night. I must mention that there were plenty of great people at the gig — most notably Charlie and his fellow band members — but the environment was a little harsh for me and I wanted to move on to our next stop which was...

OLYMPIA, WA: All I can say is that this is about the punkest town I've ever been in.

CORVALLIS, OR: We played in a coffee house to about thirty people and it was one of the best shows of the tour. There were quite a few burnt-out hippie types wandering around but most of the people were swell. Almost everyone in attendance came up and personally thanked us for playing afterwards. I think they're in dire need of more entertainment in Corvallis.

BERKELEY, CA: People's Park was a riot. Figuratively. People's Park is a dirt lot that the hippies staked out back in the '60's. It's owned by the University of California but the hippies call it their own. The University is always threatening to turn it into a volleyball court and the hippies are always trying to turn it into a comunist day care center. No compromise is ever reached so People's Park is basically a small patch of land with a few acid dealers and misguided Deadheads from out of town lurking around. We played a Save People's Park extravaganza. The hippies began by taunting the few cops that were milling around, basically begging them to arrest them. Lame folk singers and stoned poets rambled. A ridiculous lady stood up and preached to the crowd about fireworks. She told them they had to make an "inner choice" about the use of firecrackers. My "inner choice" was to bean her with a tomato but I refrained.

We played three songs. In the middle of the fourth song, a skinhead-looking guy jumped on stage and dove into my drummer's kit. I helped him off stage with the business end of the mike stand and bailed. People didn't understand why. They also don't understand why they can't keep their fucking park. I didn't feel like spelling out for them that if they sit around watching one asshole fucking with our shit like they're watching TV, it's no wonder they can't handle 500 feet of grass.

SAN FRANCISCO: I've been staying at Tim's house. Tim lives in a nice, safe yuppie neighborhood. Fine with me. I'm sick of "being punk" and staying in shit neighborhoods where people scowl and steal your shit. We played the Epcotcenter record store, which was great. My band members told me how bored they were getting sitting around in this nowhere town. Unfortunately, we can't leave quite yet because the van is totally fucked and needs work. If we're very lucky and don't eat, we may be able to afford to make it home.

Tour is pretty boring. I'm not a rock and roll kinda guy. I see a lot of bands on tour who seem to be having the time of their lives and God love 'em if it gets 'em hot. For me, however, I quickly tire of playing a gig, sleeping, getting up and driving and playing another gig to start the cycle over. It burns me out. I'm much more comfortable with going out to see a movie, sitting down to watch the ballgame with a hot dog and a beer or staying up all night writing stupid shit that nobody will ever read. If you're into touring, have fun. As for me, I'm sick of it.

I've been thinking about never playing out of town again. This is sheer laziness, but think of what fun it could be. People who really wanted to see us would have to come to our town. If they were intelligent, they could work out a schedule where they would go on tour. A different town every day, a different band every night. The main problem with that idea is that for most people it's not financially feasible. That's where frugality and communism meet.

We need a benefactor before we go any further. Someone with access to a lot of cash who can afford to buy a few buses (with toilets). I suggest MRR. Secondly, we get as many punx as possible to sign up for the punk summer tour, putting a lid of 100 people on the deal. For the entire summer, the MRR express drives these punx around to predestined punk gigs. Admission is free and the participants get paid a total of a $500.00 guarantee (supplied by charging the townies admission). This gives each person five bucks a day to eat on (this is supposed to be like a real tour as much as possible). Accommodations are entirely up to the participants; hopefully you can find a place to stay, just like a band tour. I'll personally start the ball rolling by offering a $500 guarantee to the happy MRR Readers Express next summer to see my band in Chicago.

If you haven't figured it out yet (and I'm sure most of you dummies haven't), I'm joking. I've been feeling pretty fucking alienated lately. I don't understand this whole rock star trip that every other person at a show wants to put you on, I don't understand this veganism womyn shit in which instead of attempting to educate people about our favorite issues, we alienate the fuck out of them and foster even more hostility and I definitely don't understand what's alternative about a punk scene in which the most intelligent dialogue between audience and band is, "Dude, you guys were really fuckin' great" or the ever popular "PLAY FASTER!!!" It could very well be that I'm just getting old. Or it could be that I'm getting tired of the increasing amount of people turning up to see my band that remind me so much of the people who I would have liked to kill when I was in high school.

I'm one guy in one band who doesn't want to play your fucking games. I am not interested in doing an interview for your fanzine dude and no I don't think I'd like to go to the party after the show and thanks but no thanks on the fucking autograph.

Well, I'll get over it. Just remind me to leave my brain at home next time I show up to play your town.

MAXIMUM MUSIC

What is it about being in a band that people find so exciting? Most people would probably say they just like playing music but if playing music was your goal you'd sit in a room with your guitar all day. No, I mean what is the attraction to the band experience? I can't answer that myself except to say that my life shows a marked pattern of self abuse and being in a band falls right into line with that.

Obviously people want their band to be heard and maybe they feel they will be liked and respected and given large amounts of money for entertaining others. This too makes sense, only it happens so rarely that's it difficult for me to believe that people actually think it's going to work for them. But then, the average dope always seems to think the extraordinary will happen to them. In fact, this belief seems to grow in proportion to the lack of work an individual is willing to put into a project to heighten their chances of success.

Furthermore, any thinking person must realize that even if you do run the gauntlet of fanzines, record labels and promoters needed in order to get your product out and come out of the process even half sane, the money you eventually might make is around what a hard-working assistant manager might make at a Burger King. That's certainly no incentive, or is it? I guess it's better than flipping burgers but it's definitely a lot more work and the average dope is not willing to put any work into anything besides taking a dump, getting laid or cashing a paycheck.

Speaking of getting laid, that is supposedly a good reason for getting into music. Apparently this works for some people but I can honestly say that my chances for screwing random females has not risen one iota since I picked up a guitar. Maybe I'm just ugly. But even so, this does not explain the women who get into music; everyone knows that women can get laid pretty much anytime they want to — and they can probably screw a better quality person in "civilian" life than they'll ever find in some dingy bar in South Carolina.

This is how most people seem to get into a band:

A punk kid is sitting in his bedroom in his parents' suburban home writing tunes. "These are fucking brilliant," he thinks, and he may be right. Usually though, it's the same old crap that's been done a million times before and a million times better. Still, he persists. He sees himself on a stage surrounded by adoring fans, hanging on his every word. He sees money, he sees fame, he sees big tits. So he rounds up a few friends who can sort of play instruments: a drummer who took lessons when he was twelve and might be able to borrow his cousin's set; a bass player who wants to play guitar but isn't good enough; and a guitarist who learned how to play by playing along with terrible punk records.

They batten down the hatches and begin rehearsing our hero's songs once a week in his parents' garage or basement. They start by learning lousy punk tunes by semi-popular local bands and then, as our hero gains confidence, he begins showing the band his own tunes. Within a few months they have a set full of material and are ready to play a show. They get booked on an all-ages gig and find themselves opening for a touring band with some name recognition. They're stoked. They tell all their friends to show up early to catch their set and they get to the club seven hours in advance to set up.

Once inside, they're told to shove their equipment back into a dark, hazardous crawlspace while the headlining band does a sound check. They're told they'll have twenty minutes to play their set while the soundman goes for dinner. They aren't getting paid. They don't care.

They climb onto stage and wonder why everyone except their friends is hanging around outside. They play. Nobody pays attention. They pack up and leave and no one notices. They do that roughly fifty more times over the next year. Even though no one seems to like them at first, they eventually start noticing people who aren't their friends hanging around during their set. They figure this must mean they're good. They're not. They save up their money and release a seven-inch record with terrible sound quality (due to the overpriced engineer they hired who couldn't give a fuck what they sound like) and end up with a huge pile of records sitting around. They tour and lose money because most of the shows get cancelled and the ones that don't are underattended. They still don't get it.

At this point, one of two things happens. Either the band members split up and form other bands (figuring that the only thing holding them back is not having people with the right attitude), or they actually become well known. If they split up and form other bands, these bands go nowhere just as fast as their original band. They give up and go get a real job, disillusioned with an ignorant and uncaring punk scene. If they become famous, the fun has just begun.

They start drawing larger crowds in their hometown and all their friends start begging them to get on the guest list. They put smaller bands on the bill to open for them. These bands complain about the lack of playing time and money. They harass our heroes for not going to see their band play in someone's basement two days beforehand. The promoters smell blood and start skimming at the door like a bunch of little league Bugsy Siegels. Their record label refuses to pay them. They're selling too many t-shirts to keep screening them themselves so they have to have them printed professionally. This costs more so the price per shirt rises, causing the punks to accuse them of selling out. Old fans decided their new material sucks. New fans become old fans and then disappear after deciding the band has become too popular. Audience members scream at them for not playing their favorite song, or not playing long enough. Young kids emulate them, wear their hair and clothes the same way and quote their song lyrics in angry letters to MRR.

The band inevitably gets bloated heads. Everyone is telling them they're great and their families can't bitch at them for not making money off the band anymore. They can do anything they want but they choose to do business as usual because it's easier. They become interested in expanding their musical horizons and reaching a wider audience. They only succeed in making a terrible album after trying to stretch beyond their limitations. They become annoyed at people accusing them of selling out and use that as an excuse for treating their fans like shit. Their personal comfort becomes increasingly more important to them than the values they espouse in their song lyrics. They completely lose touch with reality and at that point, they have MADE IT.

See, the people in the crowd don't want them to be like everyone else. They want them to be superhuman and the band is more than happy to try to fit the bill. They make money, the audience feels like they're part of some important cultural movement and that's that, at least until everybody gets a few years older and realizes what a ridiculous waste of time it all is.

We have an obsession with entertainment in this country, a severely unhealthy obsession. It is not easily defined; the only definition that fits is HUGE. Everything is big, big, big because we're constantly expecting someone to come along and top the next act. "IMPRESS US," we scream at the top of our lungs. We want to feel alive and we do so by living vicariously through our celebrities. It is not the act of playing in a band or painting or acting — an average nobody who is a musician, writer or actor is a piece of shit in most people's eyes unless he's on the cover of Spin or playing the blind paraplegic anti-communist double agent physician on *One Life To Live*. It is the act of being somebody in a world full of nobodies. If we can't be famous, we can at least get goddamn close to someone who is famous. We'll want to know where they were born, what their favorite flavor of ice cream is, where they stand politically, who they're fucking and what kind of car they drive. We want to know these people so well that we can tell they're JUST LIKE US, so that if we ever showed up on their doorstep they would welcome us with open arms and talk to us and do nice things for us and tell us how wonderful we are.

It's sickening of course, but we're all a part of it. We say in punk rock that we don't care about hero worship, placing people on pedestals, turning people into rock stars. But that's exactly what we want. We want to pay them to be what we're too fucking scared to be ourselves. That's why GG Allin is so popular. We aren't interested in living our own lives; we're interested in reading about how other people live their lives. We're forever watching them come through town on tour with their bands and wishing someday we could do the same but never having the balls to actually do anything about it. We want to change the world but for now we're just going to change the channel. Grab another beer and sink deeper into the grave that's waiting for you at the end of your road like a pus-oozing sore.

Being in a band is either a job or a hobby. People aren't supposed to be flabbergasted by it. Why are band members impressed by the fact that people are impressed? So they can take advantage of their ignorance and turn it into a dollar bill or a blowjob? To pump up their massive egos even more?

And what do you owe anybody who buys your records or wants to see you play? Do you owe it to them to visit their part of the country and play a show even though you don't want to? Do you owe it to them to play an hour-long set even though a half-hour set would have been better for everyone involved? I've got news for you suckers: bands sell out every day, not to Geffen or Warner's or MTV but to the hordes of obnoxious, pimply-faced little fucks who think they own you just because they bought your album. Fuck that. Being an audience member does not entitle you to tell the band how long they should play or who they should pledge their political allegiance to. If you want to confront a band on an issue, go ahead, but why waste their time with your petty little crybaby shit like "Dude, play faster!"

Being in a band is not a noble profession or even a really cool thing to do. It's generally a waste-of-time occupation filled with arrogant assholes who have been led to believe (by starry-eyed fans) that their shit doesn't stink. Instead of complaining about people being rock stars, why not just ignore them? They'll go away. Just like you will.

MAXIMUM EXTRA

There I was, hanging around watching the Cubs game on a beautiful Tuesday afternoon when my girlfriend, Portia, called from work and asked if I wanted to be an extra for a MINISTRY video. Portia works at a production studio and frequently hears about gigs for extras and since I can always use a couple of extra bucks, I'm usually interested.

A former co-worker of hers was working on this video and had told her they needed punks for some scenes the next day. Since I recently gave myself a Travis Bickle Mohawk I was a logical choice.

Being an extra is boring. Mostly you just stand around like a dope while the crew takes eight hours to set up a 30-second shot. This one would be different because the crew was not union. Also, it was low budget. Of course, "low budget" in this case meant the kind of money I could live on for about five years, but I digress.

I called the producer and asked her what the video was about. "It's sort of a post-nuclear holocaust apocalyptic sort of thing," she told me, her British accent hammering on my nerves. There's something about British accents on hipsters that I just hate. It's sort of the same way I feel about those annoying L.A. accents. Just the way they speak seems to say, "We will tolerate you cretins because we have to, but don't ever think for a second that, like us, you're on the cutting edge of radical 'ROAK MYEWZIKK!'" Actually, she turned out to be a really nice person.

Anyway, I'd get to wear a Screeching Weasel shirt and that was more important than the 30 bucks I'd get. I mean, what the hell, my own band can't afford to do a video, so why not glom onto someone else's success for a free plug? The producer was going nuts trying to get some genuine punks so I assured her that I would bring at least a few people with me.

At 9:30 the next morning, me, Portia, Dan Vapid and Brian, Doug and Rob from the Underdog crew got a cab (paid for by the producer of course) over to the first filming site. Two skinheads were running around a burning car inside a parking lot while the cameras rolled. After a couple of minutes, Al walked over to say hi.

Al is the main man in MINISTRY. If you're not familiar with MINISTRY, don't feel bad, neither am I. I know that they're one of those industrial-type dance bands and I've heard Al's name tossed around a lot in association with various "projects" but I had never heard the band before. Well, I probably had at some point — their music was used on some beer commercial — but suffice to say I'm not too knowledgeable about the band.

Anyway, Al came over and chatted with us for a minute and even offered us tickets to the Lollapalooza gig. He wore black motorcycle boots, black pants, shades and a large cowboy hat over long black dreadlocks. A scrawny goatee covered his upper lip and chin. I felt that I was in the presence of a star.

Soon, the British director called for us to come over by the car. The vehicle was set ablaze again and the disgusting-smelling smoke started pouring out of the smoke machines. We were instructed to run around the car. We did. The director called "CUT." We were asked to please not laugh or smile. We were supposed to be angry punks on a rampage, not happy go lucky goofballs making a few extra bucks by playing teenage freakshow.

The cameras started rolling again and we ran. And ran. And fucking ran. This shit was killing me. Eventually, Al walked out and began walking slowly around the car while we ran like spastic idiots around him. He looked cool. We looked totally ridiculous. I made sure to turn towards the camera as I ran by in order to flash my "billboard."

Finally, the scene was done and we bailed over to the next location. Doug rode over with Al and reported that Al drove like a madman and seemed offended when Doug told him he hadn't heard the new MINISTRY album.

Upon reaching the new location, we saw that some other punks (who had been picked up in bars and record stores the night before by the crew) had shown up, including two dykes who pawed each other relentlessly. Someone went to go get beer for Al. He was kind enough to offer some to us. I wasn't too into getting drunk at 10:30 in the morning so I declined.

A huge Winnebago was set up as a green room. It was pretty cool; the crew was treating us like real people (which doesn't often happen to an extra) and we were allowed to hang out in the green room if we wanted.

Eventually, the crew got set up and the makeup man motioned us over. He put a "bloody" bandage around my arm and fake blood on my shoulder. Then he put a huge bandage around my neck and secured it with rope, covering up my billboard. Fuck!

Everyone else got bloodied up, and then they took us down under a filthy overpass where we were told to pick up something to use as a weapon. People grabbed sticks and pipes and bottles. I got a curvy faucet head. It did not look very threatening. The smoke machines started up and the water truck started spraying the top of the overpass. We ran again. Lots and lots of running, over and over. It was getting to be a pain in the ass. I kept pulling the bandage over to uncover my billboard.

Then more hanging around. Finally, the makeup guy asked Rob and me to come up above the overpass to the train tracks. The two dykes were already up there. The dykes were to use big sticks as torches to light the "Molotov cocktails" that me and Rob were holding. Then we were to whip them down against the wall leading to the overpass. The director asked Rob to turn his Underdog Records shirt inside out. "You don't want me to turn mine around, do you?" I asked. "No," he said. "Nobody knows what Screeching Weasel is."

I pulled off the rope and stupid bandage and prepared to become a star. It took about a million times before we had the synchronization of the thing down and to tell the truth, we never really got it right. We were supposed to get the bottles lit and whip them at the same exact time. Fat chance. They finally gave up.

After that, we all went back and hid behind a large pile of dirt and garbage while we were filmed peeping up and throwing rocks and sticks until we "stormed" over the hill. According to the director, we were supposed to be fighting the National Guard. Duh.

Lunch came and it was pretty good. Free beer and soda for all, big sandwiches and a really tasty salad with little tortellini smothered in Parmesan and Romano cheese.

Then it was on to the next location, which was near Maxwell Street. That's where people sit out on the weekends selling anything you can imagine. Cassettes, stuffed animals, fruit, etc. It was like a huge garbage dump. There was shit all over the sides of the streets. I even saw a rotting dog corpse covered with hungry flies. An ice cream truck drove by and the director bought us all popsicles.

We sat around forever while the band members were filmed playing along to music amidst a background of smoke, water and garbage. I found out the video was for a tune called "New World Order" and I could hear it coming out of the little speaker held by the director. It sounded like the same note being hit over and over with a siren in the background.

In the Winnebago, I met up with this girl that hangs around at punk shows a lot. She showed me a big black fuzzy thing she was carrying around. "What the hell is that?" I asked. "Al's hair," she replied. "It fell out. I was wearing it in my hair but the producer made me take it out before Al saw it."

Yes, the man has fake hair, or hair extensions as they're called. I was shocked and embarrassed. I looked out of the back window of the Winnebago and saw Al strutting towards the camera, fake hair blowing gently in the breeze. I'd had no idea what sort of people I was dealing with. Up until this point, I had been operating under a silly illusion. The crew was so kind and worked so quickly, the band members were friendly and I had been thinking that they were all just regular folks. Wrong!

It was all downhill from there. We did some more scenes, mostly of us marching around like morons with sticks and fake guns and stuff (although Brian from 8-BARK got a cool cameo as an injured punk soldier whose wounds were being soothed by two very nice looking girls) but my heart just wasn't in it. I mean, here we were in a predominantly black, poor neighborhood, shooting scenes for some crap video (with cops to protect us from the locals) and for what? It was a fucking load of shit; some guy with phony hair trying to tell the world that angry punks were going to storm the streets after the shit hits the fan with the new world order? Gimme a break. The punks will be hiding away in some warehouse, listening to lousy music and swilling cheap beer. And of course, they had to show the guitarist and bass player jamming (without amps of course), as if in the middle of this huge riot, the members of MINISTRY are going to be dressing up in their silly black clothes and walking around playing their tunes in front of a condemned building.

After we were done for the day, Vapid asked Al about those Lollapalooza tickets. Al's wife took over, saying it was very unlikely because the people running the show were such assholes.

Oh well. That's rock and roll.

MAXIMUM LIARS

"OK Ben, how old are you?"
"24."
"Well you have to be 25 so I'm going to put 25 down. How much money do you make?"
"Ummm, about five thousand a year."
"Ok, you need to make at least thirty-five thousand to get in."
"Alright, thirty-five."
"What do you do for a living?"
"Uhhh... how about a teacher?"
That's good. Where did you graduate from and what kind of a degree do you have?"
"Let's say I have a B.A. in... liberal arts! Yeah... and I got it from NIU."

It went on like this for another few minutes. I was in a delicious sweat from all the lies she was encouraging me to tell. This was going to be fun.

In addition to the information about my finances, age and schooling, it was necessary for me to be a drinker of imported beer both at home and in bars as well as a connoisseur of microbrewery products (both with an anally particular frequency). Plus, I was supposed to have drank Guinness Stout on tap at least twice in the past week but not out of the bottle in the past month. Crazy. Of course, it helps to have someone in charge of screening participants who doesn't give a flying fuck what you do as long as you make up the correct information.

When I was done with the twenty minutes screening process I mentioned that my roommate would be interested in being part of the group as well.

"OK," she said. "We'll change the college, occupation and address and leave everything else the same as yours." We were now officially part of a focus group.

The group was to meet at 5:30 the next day in the offices of a slick new building downtown. I shaved, put deodorant under my stinky pits and dug out a nice red sweater I save for weddings and funerals. Vapid and I caught the El downtown and made our way through a sea of glassy-eyed yuppies.

"Wait five minutes before you come in," I told him. "We're not supposed to know each other."

Vapid looked nervous. "What if they bust me?"

"Don't worry about it. I told you, they're just going to ask some random questions from the list. Just remember who you're supposed to be."

I looked back over my shoulder and saw him fidgeting in the middle of the sidewalk. Vapid fidgets a lot. I felt a bit like a mother leaving her child for the first day of kindergarten. He'll handle it, I thought. Vapid isn't used to lying but he'd learn that 90% of bullshitting a corporate executive type is acting like you own the goddamn place no matter how crazy you sound.

The elevator deposited me two feet in front of the receptionist's desk. I told her my name and she began asking random questions off a stack of papers on the desk. I passed the second screening and was invited to take a seat in the waiting room. Perching my ass on a plush couch, I browsed through the latest *U.S. News And World Report*. Boring. I noticed a tray full of tasty looking little deli sandwiches just as another woman came out and instructed me to eat up.

"You'll be drinking beer so you might want to have something in your stomach."

I agreed and grabbed a couple of turkey and tomatoes. A big jocko Jim Belushi looking guy sat at the other end of the room and tried to make small talk. I stuffed my mouth with poultry meat to avoid answering.

The guy who got me the gig, Cal, came in. We weren't supposed to know each other. Playing the game 100%, he asked me what I did for a living.

"Teacher," I mumbled through a mouthful of bird. Belushi looked impressed.

I heard Vapid come in. The receptionist asked him questions that I couldn't make out, but I could hear his answers.

"Yeah. Yeah. Well... Yeah." His voice oozed anxiety. "Ummm... sometimes. Yeah, in a nutshell."

In a NUTSHELL??? I bit the insides of my cheeks. Vapid, having somehow convinced the receptionist that he wasn't utterly full of shit, sauntered over to the couch carrying a roast beef delectable. He made sure to sit a reasonable distance away from me.

"Mind if I smoke?" I asked. Everyone shook his head. I fired up a Kool just as HE entered.

His face was pink and well scrubbed. A small colony of zits were visible on his neck, up until the point where his collar held to his skin as if welded there. A yellow and blue spotted tie hung down and he adjusted it with his smooth, well-manicured fingers. Three hundred dollar shoes, impeccably pressed pants, haircut by Wall Street. He looked like he'd just stepped out of a Rob Lowe movie. A real, live yuppie. I'd never been as close to one as I was at that moment.

I was distracted from this unusual sight as a tall, thin bearded man walked into the waiting room holding a clipboard.

"I'm Steve," he said. His British accent was at once both pleasing and repulsive to my ears. "It looks like we're a few short but we're going to forge ahead anyway. Follow me."

He led us to a large table inside a conference room. I took the chair at the foot of the table, placing the name card he had so thoughtfully provided neatly in front of me. Vapid sat to my right, the yuppie man next to him. On my left was Belushi and next to him, Cal.

Steve asked who would like to tell the group about themselves. My hand shot up. I was EAGER for this.

"My name is Ben," I said. "I teach fifth grade science down at John Marsh on the South Side." The teacher lie, like all great lies, was slightly based in reality. An ex-Screeching Weasel bass player actually holds that very position.

"And what are your drinking habits, Ben?" Steve was so polite. The perfect Brit.

"Well, I'm a Guinness man. I usually stop by the tavern in the late afternoon, after I've finished grading papers. I like to have a quick Guinness, then maybe pick up a six-pack of Beck's at the liquor store before heading home."

Vapid's eyes were fairly bugged. I went on. "I go out to clubs occasionally. I'll usually start with a Guinness or two..."

Belushi piped in, "They're real filling — I can only drink a couple." Steve gently directed the action back to me. "Do you find that you switch brands after a while?"

"Yeah," I said eagerly. "The Guinness really fills you up. It's like eating a meal." I've never touched the goddamn shit in my life. I took a chance. "They're real high in alcohol content. I usually switch to Beck's or Heineken after a couple of Guinness."

Steve was very pleased. "Yes, we've done this survey on the West Coast in six cities and everyone seems to agree on that point."

Introductions went around the table ending with Vapid, whose lies about being a Columbia graduate and professional sound engineer fell weakly from his lips.

The action moved on. We were shown several different advertising slogans written in plain black type on poster boards. We agreed which ones were best by consensus, myself and Cal leading the bullshit brigade the entire way. Belushi was a real bigmouth. He kept butting in, which wasn't so bad, but he wasn't a very good liar. Several times he succeeded in bringing the discussion to a standstill with his overstated falsehoods.

Steve must've thought Vapid was shy. I really believe the Brit never considered that young Vapid might be lying through his teeth. He kept bringing it back to the poor guy. I wanted to tell Vapid to just speak up a little more in order to avoid being asked so many questions, but of course I couldn't.

Steve's eyes now rested on Vapid.

"Dan," he said. "You say that you like to drink three or four Guinness when you go out. That's a little higher than everyone else. I was wondering, is that pints or half-pints?"

Vapid froze, the proverbial deer in the headlights. I swear I saw a small bead of sweat form at his forehead. "Well..." he said. All eyes were on him. Yuppie-man was leaning forward in his chair. My God, I thought. Of course! He doesn't know what a pint is! This is a guy who drinks Miller out of cans. He doesn't have the money to be hanging around in hip taverns ordering up pints of ale and stout. HE DOESN'T KNOW! Now I'm getting nervous. Steve is getting a confused look on his face. Finally, slowly, Vapid speaks.

"It depends."

And it was received like the Holy Grail. Anything short of "Fuck it, you busted me, I'm a bald-faced liar!" would have gotten a standing ovation. It was a breeze from then on. We were given about 20 different bottles of beers and were asked to work together to arrange them into three different sections. There was some difficulty when Steve asked Vapid why he grouped a blond beer with an ale (Vapid later confessed that he didn't know what a blond beer was and hell, I didn't really know either, but the ability to define words contextually has saved my lying ass more than once). Yuppie-man insisted that we were all wrong. He was beginning to understand that he was the only person in the room who even came close to actually fitting the criteria required to enter this sacred circle. I really think that motherfucker must've answered every screening question with complete and total honesty, and actually fit the bill. His obvious discomfort and confusion entertained the hell out of me.

Eventually, the beer was brought in. We were each given our own bottles and cups and were asked to comment. The first beer was actually pretty good. It had that microbrew, thick taste to it at first, but then went down light like a pilsner. The second beer was a bit stronger and had an unpleasant, stale aftertaste. The third was way strong. Like the kind of beer that farmers in English pubs might drink. Everyone but Yuppie-man voted the first, wimpy, American-tasting beer as the favorite.

Yuppie-man had had enough. "You guys seem to like those weak beers so much. I mean, I don't know about you, but I LIKE Guinness! You all say you drink it so often, so how can you like that first one? It tastes like OLD STYLE!"

Asshole. I like Old Style. Steve was gentle with him. "Well, I guess Andrew likes his beer a bit stronger, men!" Andrew gave it up soon after. After all the time he must've spent patronizing the shit out of anyone viewed as lesser than him during his offensive lifetime, it must have really pissed him off to receive the same treatment.

We were asked what we would call this kind of beer, what kind of images it conjured up. I was getting slightly buzzed, as we had been invited to finish all three beers. I rarely drink more than one or two at a sitting, and this stuff was strong.

"It makes me think of nighttime," I mused. "Maybe something with twilight or midnight in the name. Like Midnight Moon or something." Steve looked surprised and pleased, though I don't know why. I mean, would you buy a beer called frigging Midnight Moon? It sounds like a Tony Bennett song or something. But I was on a roll. "The name would have to appeal to women," I said. "See, this beer is like a stout, but not as filling. It has definite feminine appeal." Belushi and Cal were egging me on now, little cries of agreement coming from their lying mouths and corny "I-think-we're-on-to-something" looks plastered all over their sweaty faces.

"Yes!" I shouted, pounding my fist on the table. "Upscale women will love this beer. They'll be able to keep up with their boyfriends in the bar." Noticing the video camera and crew of employees behind the poorly designed two-way mirror, I decided to get scientific. "We all know that women's stomachs have thinner lining than men's, enabling them to feel the effects of alcohol quicker and with more intensity than us, right?" Everyone except Yuppie-man harumphed their agreement. "Well, we market this as an alternative to the heavy stout: Midnight Moon — or maybe twilight something — it doesn't matter — GREAT STOUT TASTE THAT WON'T SEND YOU HOME IN A CAB AT MIDNIGHT! Or something to that effect." I sat back in my chair and folded my hands. I considered putting my feet on the table.

"Guys," I reflected. "This is gonna be huge."

The other guys ran with the ball for a while and then we were thanked by Steve and escorted out. On the way to the elevator, we were handed white envelopes, each containing a crisp fifty-dollar bill. Vapid and I laughed all the way home.

MAXIMUM PUNK & PROFIT MARGINS

I've spent so much time spouting off about major labels you'd think I wouldn't have anything more to say. Of course I do.

First of all, I'd like to extend a big kick in the pants to anyone who is actually stupid enough to believe that major labels moving in and buying up punk rock is a big deal. That is not a big deal, not at all. Major labels exist to make money. It wouldn't matter if they were selling dildos or kewpie dolls — their bottom line is profit. I guess we could all wring our hands and wrinkle up our foreheads in concern over the fact that these leeches exist, but I personally don't have the time for such fantastic horseshit.

The problem isn't major labels coming in to the punk scene to buy up your favorite bands. How can they buy something that's not for sale? And if it is for sale, what do you care? See, there are three classes of bands. There are the bands that wouldn't dream of selling out and can afford that luxury of ethics because they have such a tiny cult audience that nobody's asking them to sell out. Then there are the bands (and I'll tell ya, my town is crammed full of 'em) that use the D.I.Y. ethic first as an excuse for creating an arrogant, elitist club and then as a stepping-stone towards becoming the next Bad Religion. Then there are the bands that fall somewhere in the middle. These are the bands that really believe in and own their ethics but are not stupid or naive enough to believe that playing five-dollar gigs in V.F.W. halls is going to be satisfying for them in another five years. There are other classes of bands of course, like all the shitty bar rock and pop bands that were sending their demo tapes to major labels years ago and are now calling themselves alternative and getting signed by the truckload. I won't concern myself with them because they are the mainstream segment of our population. They are the Van Halen's of the '90s, eternally clueless, forever stuck in a high school locker room gauging the length of everyone else's prick to make sure they don't fall short.

I'm sure many of the other writers in MRR have a wide range of opinions and ideas about what we should do about this. But really, why should anybody do anything about it? Bands that are gonna sell out are gonna do it regardless of what anyone says. The only thing that bugs me about that is that they never have the balls to admit they sold out. They're always justifying it in silly, pathetic ways, as if they actually need to retain their credibility with the punks.

I used to get pissed about bands that used the structure I supported and believed in to get what they wanted, only to drop the punk scene. I don't care as much anymore because that's the norm now. Lookout Records never used to make bands sign contracts. Now they have to because so many of their bands show the telltale signs of jumping ship. Lookout needs to protect itself. Yeah, it's fucked, but that's what's happened.

It doesn't matter to me because I'm so rarely inspired by punk music these days anyway. It's interesting to note, however, that the best punk rock being made today is coming out of Spain, Germany and Italy. Some of the greatest bands I've heard in the past year will never play in this country and will never have their records sold here. Certainly part of the reason for this is because they don't have the opportunities that we Americans do to sell out. I definitely don't think those circumstances are good. I think the whole situation sucks. Bands like Spain's Shock Treatment and Depressing Claim are much better than most of the bands on say, Epitaph or Lookout, and they won't sell one tenth of the records that their American counterparts do. That sucks. But on the other hand, even though many of these bands are heavily influenced by popular American bands, their lack of a solid, easy ten-step program to success means they have the freedom to do exactly what they want. It's doubtful that any but a few of the great, unknown European punk bands see themselves as having the slightest chance to become famous — therefore, what they do is more pure in intent and more honest in execution. It's impossible for them to pander to an audience because they basically don't have one, at least not in the way that we think of it.

I would never suggest that this makes them better people, or more ethical than their American counterparts. Surely if they had access to the same easy program of success that we do, they'd fall prey to the same shit we do. But the parallel is in the American bands of the late eighties who were in a similar situation.

We had some heavy hitters around back then, even though their glory days were long over. Circle Jerks, 7 Seconds, M.D.C. and probably about ten others were still capable of drawing huge crowds wherever they went. But great punk bands that were just starting out got virtually no support. Of course, many of these bands went on to be legendary, but how many people remember that when Operation Ivy came to Chicago, they played in front of about 100 people? Most of the punks were off at the Agnostic Front show. The same could be said for Crimpshrine, Jawbreaker, Cringer and countless others who are revered today. Now, a great young band like Face To Face or Propagandhi can go out on tour and you can bet your ass they'll be drawing huge crowds. That's not a bad thing by any means — it just shows that the punks have finally caught on. There's no doubt in my mind that a bill featuring NOFX and Face To Face would draw hundreds more people than an Exploited gig, but it wasn't too long ago that NOFX couldn't draw flies and Face To Face didn't even exist.

Unfortunately, what has come along with this is the tendency of younger bands to see their music in a purely business sense. I don't mean just money — I'm talking about the underlying attitude these bands have. As is the case with just about everyone on the planet, it seems that most young bands live in a black and white world; either you sell your records only through small indie distributors or you go for the brass ring sporting the Bad Religion logo. We've seen bands like Husker Du ruined by going for the gold and we've seen other bands like 7 Seconds turn to shit by being naive and ignorant about business. You would think that bands would've learned from all that and found some middle ground, but most haven't.

Jawbreaker is one of the few bands that have. These guys aren't dummies when it comes to business. They're also not crooks. Moreover, they have a sense of fun about what they do that goes beyond the usual definition of the word. While half the punk scene is calling them sell-out scumbags and the other half is wondering why they haven't made the "smart" move and signed to a major, they're cruising along doing business as usual. Their ethics are their own. Don't tell me it's easy for a band like Jawbreaker to do what they do. No, it's easy for some podunk, nobody band to take an ethical stand. Just about every major label around has approached Jawbreaker and they've turned them all down. How many young bands do you know who would do the same?

But Jawbreaker are not going to be suckered into a no-win situation with a club that's going to stiff them or a kid promoter with twisted D.I.Y. ethics who thinks that anything above gas money is immoral. They do their business by their own rules and I respect and admire them for that. Yet while every other band in the country is attempting to rip off their sound, few, if any, are attempting to understand the way Jawbreaker does business, which is ultimately what gained them their popularity and is probably what keeps them going. The mere fact that they're one of only two bands I can name (the other being NOFX) that actually gets considerably better with each record should say something. It doesn't have anything to do with marketing or politics; it has to do with priorities.

Mykel mentioned in his April column that Screeching Weasel had signed with Warner Bros. A lot of people asked me if this was true which was not only an insult in itself, but also a sign of people's general stupidity; if you don't take everything Mykel says in his April column with a grain of salt, you're not too bright.

What pissed me off wasn't so much people asking me if it was true (when what they should have been saying is "What kind of bullshit is Mykel talking about?") although that bugged me slightly. I also wasn't all that annoyed by the people who gloated over it, as if their silly predictions had finally come true, although that was slightly annoying as well. What really irritated the shit out of me were the people who believed it and thought it was an intelligent and logical move.

Look, I don't really give a fuck for the punk scene today. I don't know what you call it when you're miles past jaded and disillusioned, but that's where I am. I have only a few reasons for retaining the slight interest I do in punk rock. But signing to a major? Come on! I won't talk ethics here, because if somebody threw enough money at me I'd leave my ethics behind in a New York minute. Let's just talk business.

If you're going to sign to a major, you first have to have interest from the majors. We have very little. Without that interest, you can't get yourself the deal you want.

Secondly, you have to be willing to accept the fact that the people you're dealing with don't give a fuck if you end up on welfare or shoot shit into your arm or blow your fucking head off with a shotgun. In fact, those people will exploit any problems you may have, romanticize them and leave your silly ass twisting in the wind.

Third, no matter how good you think you are you'll probably flop and, unlike most punk indies, major labels don't care if you're a really good band or not. If you're not making money, fuck you, and pal, once you've taken that road you can't go back. Your career as a musician is over.

Fourth, even if you become huge, the fuckers steal from you. You'll be making so much money it won't matter but you will be getting robbed (this last one is unfortunately true of many indies as well).

Fifth, in order to protect yourself as much as possible, you have to give a cut of your dough to a lot of people who aren't doing nearly enough to earn it (and don't forget that there are many more salaries to pay and everybody wants, and gets, a piece of your action).

Last, you have to do things. You can get a contract saying you don't have to do videos or you only have to tour one month a year but if you stick with that shit, you'll flop. If you sell 60,000 albums on Lookout, you'll be set for at least a few years, assuming your needs and tastes are like that of the average Joe. If you sell 60,000 albums on Atlantic, it's unlikely that you'll see a dime and if you're lucky, they might give you one more chance to make some real money before they drop you like a bad habit.

So from a purely financial standpoint, I don't think I'm capable of doing such stuff. I mean, I feel like I'm in on the world's greatest scam or something. I get paid what I think is an obscene amount of money and all I have to do is what I'd be doing anyway — writing and recording songs and going out to play them in front of people once in a while. Even when my band breaks up, I'll most likely continue to make money because nothing jacks up record sales like a band breaking up (or one of the members O.D.ing or eating a shotgun shell).

Financially, I'm the first to admit that I'm pretty cynical. I don't try to justify the money I make by saying that I'm giving something important to people or making the world a better place. There are many better bands with far more intelligent people running them that will never make the kind of money I'm making (and let's clear something up here before the more reactionary among you start flipping out — I make about $15,000 a year. In the real world, that ain't shit for a 26-year-old man. Unless of course you're like me and have no other skills besides pumping gas and hauling boxes onto trucks, in which case, as far as I'm concerned, I'm one wealthy sonofabitch). I got lucky. I don't press my luck. I'm no gambler and a deal with a major is nothing more than a high stakes crap shoot.

Green Day is showing all the signs of becoming the next Nirvana, or damn close. I'm happy for them. I wouldn't have done it their way but it seems to be working out for them. But what about all the other bands that have signed recently? Does anybody really believe that Samiam is actually going to break through to a mainstream audience? How about Jawbox? And what about all the bands that are secretly hoping that the day will come when they get to take that crap shoot? If I was a nice guy, I'd feel sorry for them. But I'm not a nice guy and I won't cry any tears when they lose everything that was ever important to them.

The punk scene has grown up. We shouldn't be acting so goddamned stupid now. We know better. I'm not going to condemn anyone who signs to a major. Their business is their own. But if you're going to sell out, at least do it smart. Admit you've sold out. Don't be naive enough to believe that major labels have changed to fit the punks. Get a good lawyer and never forget that you have no friends at the label, that they'll kick you out on your ass if you don't turn a profit. Don't forget that the ones who are signing your paychecks are also stealing a hefty chunk of your profit. Don't forget that your lifespan as a band will be considerably shortened and you'll likely turn to some form of dope or end up with an ulcer from all the pressure to do more and be more. And most importantly, don't forget that your success or failure has nothing to do with how good you are or how smart you are. It has to do with factors that nobody can explain, just like shooting craps. If you go into it ready to lose everything you have, you might come out of it relatively undamaged. Me, I think I'll leave the dice tossing to those with more nerve.

MAXIMUM ISMS

Author's note: "Maximum Isms" was written in response to a MaximumRockNRoll staffer who quit the magazine in protest over what he felt were anti-homosexual and racist comments made by one of the other columnists. He wrote a whiny column explaining why he was quitting — I offered a parody.

Welcome to the MRR columns section, the only part of the magazine that doesn't think discourse & expression of differing opinions = fascism. By now you've had enough of the multitude of reactionary gay white male crybabies (who have a real understanding of women's issues since they happen to enjoy having sex with men) nervously defending their standards that seem to hang around the scene like stale farts, so settle down and get ready for some faggot-hating, misogynist, ultra-defensive, macho chest-beating, right-wing mania.

To begin with, I'm pulling out the war club and demanding to know why I was placed LAST in the columns section of two issues ago. We all know that Tim generally puts what he thinks are the best columns first. The lousier columns end up in the back. But I don't know if I've ever seen a regular columnist actually placed behind a guest column! Did it suck that bad? I demand a recount! What about this one? Where will it be placed? Perhaps if I mention Jello or Ian a few times, I'll get moved up. Mebbe if I ramble about the anarchists I'll get a better slot. But wait! I know as well as you that column-placement isn't the issue here. I know that you go on a manic search for my column when you get your copy of this rag. I know nothing will deter you from seeking out my words of wisdom like a rabid dog for a fibula. The issue here is not one of inflammation. I speak not of my hemorrhoids, which have troubled me not at all since spring, but of writing a column to generate some much-needed hate mail.

Now, I could say FAG a lot. Even though it's just a word, even though I could use it only in a dumb name-calling context that has nothing to do with sexual preference, even though bothering to react to it would be like bothering to write in and accuse a columnist of being insensitive to the low-I.Q.ed for using the word "retard," it's still got quite a bite. Fuck, I could probably get one of the staffers to quit over it!

But I'm not gonna do that. I'm tired of making people angry. I don't want you to be my enemy. I want you to be my friend. We're all in this together. It takes 484 muscles to smile and only 11 to frown, so smiling is good exercise! Of course, it takes 643 muscles to kick the stupid smile off of some motherfucker's face so that's better exercise... wait, stop, strike that immediately! I'm being bad again. Punk isn't about being bad. Punk isn't about being insensitive. Punk isn't about hurting other people's feelings. What have I been saying all these years? What was I writing in the preceding paragraphs? I KNOW what punk's about. It's about respecting each other's rights. It's about being kind to your fellow man (unless that fellow man happens to be a white male reactionary anti-choice conservative middle class right wing religious heterosexual fuckhead in which case we should fuck up his system, pronto). Everything I've written in MRR up until this very paragraph has been nothing but an outgrowth of my own fucked-up upbringing into a patriarchal society by conservative, anti-choice, pro-death penalty, misogynist, homophobic WHITE MALES. Well, I don't want your hate mail. I'm changing my tune.

I hereby ask... wait, I started that wrong. Gimme a break. I'm still learning. AHEM. I hereby DEMAND that all MRR readers, hell, all PUNKS stop using the words "crazy," "nuts," "mental," "wacked," "wingnut" or any other derogatory word used to describe mental illness. You see, I have a mental disorder known as PANIC DISORDER or GENERALIZED ANXIETY DISORDER or AGORAPHOBIA (no, these aren't band names. Stop having fun and pay attention to what I'm saying, goddamnit!). I see a shrink. I'm on medication. I've got a mental problem that I honestly wouldn't wish on my worst enemy. And I'm tired of these hurtful words being thrown around. I wanna kill every time somebody says the word "crazy" or "insane." How the heck do you think that bullcrud makes me feel as a person?

I'll tell you how it makes me feel. It pisses me off, damnit. I'm tired of MY PEOPLE, the mentally ill, being the whipping boys and grrrls for closed-minded punks who think that mental illness is funny, or worse, some sort of character defect. I WAS BORN THIS WAY! I CAN'T CHANGE IT! STOP FUCKING WITH ME! Oh yes, we're easy to pick on. Nobody wants to admit to having mental problems so we hide, afraid, chuckling along with all the jokes about that fellow who works the drill press over in the corner, he's crazy, man! HA HA FUCKING HA! What I REALLY wanna do is LASH THE FUCK OUT and put these goddamn MENTALLY STABLE people in their fucking place but I can't because I live in an intolerant, fucked-up society, a society that is ultimately afraid of me and my people.

I know what you're thinking, asshole. You're thinking, why doesn't he stop it? Why must he add to the list of ISMs that already plague us? Well, WE ARE PEOPLE TOO! We COULD accept the fact that we have to change people's minds slowly and in the meantime learn how to live in an intolerant society. We COULD accept the fact that everybody's got a cross to bear, that everybody's life sucks in one way or another and we're not the only ones suffering as did Job in the Old Testament. But FUCK that. We are going to demand change RIGHT NOW from EVERYONE effective IMM-FUCKING-EDIATELY!!! (Please contact me via MRR if you wish to join up with my new direct-action organization, NUT NATION. We're currently fucking up sane people's shit left and right. There may be jail time involved in some of our revolutionary hijinx so the timid need not apply!)

You as a true punk need to call people on their shit. Tossing around words like "nuts" and "wacko" is NOT FUCKING FUNNY! ONLY US MENTALLY ILL PEOPLE ARE ALLOWED TO USE THOSE WORDS! You don't like my band? Well it's not because you don't like the music. It's not because you think we write lousy lyrics. It's not because we're just not good. IT'S BECAUSE YOU DON'T UNDERSTAND THE PLIGHT OF THE MENTALLY ILL!!! YOU JUST DON'T GET IT! You closed-minded suburban middle-class mentality assholes are not hip to the radical nutcase experience! Sheesh, what fucking SQUARES you are! I've got a word for you people. SANERS. That's an insult! You saners think you can force your bullshit, uptight, clear-minded way of thinking on the rest of us, well FUCK YOU FUCK YOU FUCK YOU! WE'RE SICK AND GODDAMNED TIRED OF BEING HELD DOWN BY YOU FUCKERS! Do you have any idea of the abuse that goes on in state mental hospitals? Do you even care? If you do, where do you think that comes from? It comes from all your fucking insensitive stupid anti-mentally ill jokes, that's where. You're fucking nutsophobic. In fact, I think the whole goddamn MRR staff (except for us columnists) is nutsophobic. You just watch! Tim will place this column in the back of the section. If he doesn't, it'll only be because he's too scared to stand up and face my wrath as a PROUD CRAZYMAN!

Well, this is just getting to be too much for me! WE'RE HERE, WE'RE WEIRD, GET USED TO IT! If Tim does not institute a NO NUTSOPHOBIA rule for all the reactionary, backwards, straight-laced SANERS out there, I'm quitting. That's right, I'm taking my fucking ball and going home. It's my goddamn column and I'll cry if I want to.

THE NANNY AND THE ROCK STAR

The call came in sometime in the early morning hours. I do not answer my phone in the early morning hours. The machine does. The caller, chummy enough with me to know my home number, yet not enough of a pal to leave his name, instead left the following message: "I just heard that Jawbreaker is doing a week in the southwest with Nirvana and Mudhoney so I guess that shoots your theory to shit, doesn't it, pal?"

I heard the message when I woke up in the morning. An hour later I got a call from Pfahler.

"You won't believe what happened," he said.

"You're doing a week with Nirvana and Mudhoney in the southwest," I answered, fairly pleased with myself.

"Jesus," he said. "WE only found out yesterday..."

It isn't too surprising. Jawbreaker's many detractors in the punk scene have been waiting for something like this; an apparent chink in the armor. Those who publicly declare their affinity for the band are subjected to cryptic late night phone calls from anonymous Puritans. In punk rock, bad news travels fast, and rumors and gossip move at the speed of light. Good news, by the way, doesn't travel at all.

The leg of the tour that Jawbreaker would be on — despite my midnight caller's assertion to the contrary — would not be confined to the southwest. Jawbreaker did six shows with Nirvana — two in Chicago. I was provided with the opportunity to document the backstage goings on at a big time rock show, a chance I couldn't pass up as a tenacious Panic Button reporter.

I don't know if the tour was worth Jawbreaker's time, or the grief they had to put up with from hard-line punks. As for me, I'm a reporter and I go where the story is. Even if I have to dig one up.

We arrive at the Aragon Ballroom around 3:00 P.M. As we attempt to pull the van into the parking lot reserved for band vehicles, we're stopped by a stereotypical Chicago mook who asks the threatening yet polite-sounding question, "CAN I HELP YOU?" Chris spends a few minutes conversing with the guy and finally convinces him that we are indeed authorized to park in the lot. We pull up next to the two big tour buses rented by Nirvana. They have been christened "Wave Dancer" and "Blue Mirage," complete with cheesy airbrush paintings on the back that have me wondering if Loretta Lynn might be making a guest appearance tonight. The people from the catering truck pay no attention to us as we file into the building from the alley entrance. We head for the Jawbreaker dressing room, a drab little white-walled hole. There aren't many people around, save for the occasional security thug and the caterers, who are busy preparing the meal for the night.

I walk out onto the balcony of the dressing room and look down at the few Nirvana fans who are already camped outside the club. The El train rushes by every ten minutes. Boring. I am here to get a scoop. The boys have already warned me that my chances are slim, but I'm certain that my charm and determination will get me SOMETHING to write about. I vow to keep my scoop antennae up throughout the entire debacle.

Bill — Jawbreaker's roadie — suggests that we visit Nirvana's tour manager to get a pass for yours truly and to demand extra beer for the evening. We worm our way through a labyrinth of dark walkways back to the office of the man in charge of the tour, Jeff. Jeff is on the phone, so we sit down and wait, chatting with Karina, head caterer. Once we have Jeff's attention, Bill and Chris mention my need for a pass (it would be taken care of later), turn in the guest list (which would go through fifty miles of red tape before reaching the front door; the people running the tour all have laptop computers and walkie talkies. Instead of simply walking the guest list downstairs, they have to put it into the computer and route it through Dante's Inferno and back before it reaches the hands of the Will Call people) and mention the fact that another twelve-pack would be nice. Giving a fatherly grin, Jeff asks, "Do you really need all that beer?" Apparently this is in reference to the fact that Chris has gotten severely blasted at several of the shows prior to today. Chris assures him that we do indeed need all that beer and Jeff, sighing heavily, says he'll do his best.

Now it's time to explore and Bill, having been at the Aragon for the show two days prior, agrees to show me around. We inspect every corner of the building, constantly discovering neat little things I'd never noticed in my previous visits to the Aragon. The stage left balcony, for instance, is closed off for people with backstage passes. This is where the caterers prepare the meal and set up the dinner table. Later, it will serve as seating for the privileged few with the all-important passes.

The stage is set up for Nirvana. Two mannequins that have been mutated into resembling the figure on the cover of the new Nirvana album flank the stage. Bits of shrubbery and other knick-knacks are glued here and there. The band's amps and speaker cabinets are covered over with red velvet cloth; set up in front of them are tiny Marshall practice amps. What a bunch of funny guys. Bill remarks that so far, not a single audience member has seemed to notice or understand Nirvana's wacky sight gag.

Bill and I head to the floor, which we discover has recently been waxed, making it a perfect skating rink. We skate around for a while (and of course, nobody bugs us; when you BELONG in a joint like this, you can get away with just about anything) like a couple of idiots.

As I glide towards the stage, I hear Blake yell my name from the balcony, and at the same time, a small rectangular box hits the floor next to me. A-ha! It's my Kools. One of the perks, you see, of being on a big tour like this is that before the show, a gopher will run and get the bands and crew certain necessities, like aspirin, moist towellettes, or smokes. For me it's free Kools. It's already been worth my while to show up.

Our ears are suddenly assaulted by a deafening blast of white noise from the stage monitors. Apparently this is how professional sound people test their gear. It's horrifying, but nowhere near as bad as the gigantic Scot with a mohawk and three square miles of tattoos who then proceeds to test Cobain's amp by playing the riff from "Godzilla" (read: "Smells Like Teen Spirit") complete with very metal guitar solos. I wonder if the massive mohican knows all the solos from *Purple Rain*; practically the entire predominantly Scottish crew worked on the last Prince tour. Is British labor just cheaper?

I go back to my skating competition with Bill and literally just about run into a kid who has come in from the side entrance. He introduces himself as a former member of the Lonely Trojans, a now-defunct college pop-punk band from downstate. He has managed to sneak in to get an interview with Mudhoney, Nirvana's primary support band for the tour. No one from Mudhoney is around. He follows us around for a while and then loses interest and goes back outside, asking us to make sure to try to get him in when the fabled Mudhoney shows up. Hearing the tail end of his plea, Adam remarks, "Fuck that." Um, OK.

Back in the dressing room, I am handed my pass. It's a laminated doohickey featuring a photo of a man dressed in lingerie lying in a bathtub, the word "PRINCESS" scrawled across his belly in black Sharpie. At the bottom, the pass reads "VIP." I am told that this pass is second only to the all-access passes that the bands and crew get and one or two steps above the passes that friends and relatives get. I can go anywhere backstage except for Nirvana's dressing room. I place the pass around my neck, determined to exploit my first and probably last backstage pass for as long as I can.

We are told that dinner is ready. We sit down at the end of the long table on the balcony and are given a variety of choices for a main course, including, according to Johnny, one of the caterers, "Eggplant, artichoke hearts, red onions and parmesan, lamb chops with baby onions, mushrooms and mint pesto, roast turkey with mustard sauce, salmon with roast pepper salsa and a pumpkin herb Swiss cheese goulet." I don't know what that last one is and neither does Johnny. In addition to all this, there are salads, cheese and crackers, various breads, pastries and cookies and a variety of sodas, bottled water and Gatorade.

I ask Karina if the salmon has any bones in it.

"I already told you it's a fillet," she exclaims in her thick Scottish accent.

"A what??"

"A fillet!"

She looks at me as if I may be a bit retarded. I'm utterly confused. Blake jumps in.

"Ben, she means 'fill-ay'," he says, pronouncing it correctly instead of phonetically. Now I get it. I ask whence the fish came. Karina is getting frustrated.

"I don't know," she says between clenched teeth. "Would you like to know which waters it swam in?"

Johnny tells me it's Alaskan. Karina peers at me as if deciding whether or not to clobber me over the head.

The meal is excellent, mispronunciations and thinly-veiled hostility notwithstanding.

Mudhoney finally shows up and Bill tells them that there's someone outside who wants to interview them. One of them looks out the dressing room window and says, laughing, "I don't know him." He walks away. But not far enough away. The band member and his tour manager have staked out the Jawbreaker dressing room, talking loudly. Tape recorder in hand, I approach them.

"You guys are from Seattle, huh?" I say brightly.

Mr. Mudhoney gets all serious like I'm doing some sort of important interview.

"Yeah," he answers.

"What did you think of the Mariners this year?"

Mr. M ponders this one for a moment.

"Y'know, the Mariners, baseball... are you a fan?"

"Uh, no, not really. I saw Gaylord Perry's 300th win. And I saw one game this year. Griffey hit a home run but I missed it 'cause I was walking around."

"What about the Seahawks?" I ask, grinning like an escaped lunatic.

"I don't follow football too much. I heard they're doing OK this year."

Now I'm wondering why the hell the poor guy downstairs even wanted to interview these chumps. I sit back down as the manager starts blabbering about his father who was a mountain climber. I am not impressed. What the fuck kind of a sport is mountain climbing? Seeing that I've turned off the recorder, the two imbeciles resume their inane conversation, talking way too loud, as they've already consumed a few beers. Why the hell they don't go next door to their own dressing room is a mystery to me, until I peek down the hallway and see that every scumbag leech in the history of the Chicago music scene is already next door hobnobbing with the other knobs that comprise Mudhoney.

Sitting back down in the chair, I ponder the fact that Jawbreaker doesn't seem too keen on these geeks being in their dressing room. In fact, they'd told me earlier that the other night they'd walked into the room to find Mudhoney standing around smoking pot. Fucking hippies.

I lean forward in my chair and say loudly, "I'M FROM CALIFORNIA!"

The conversation stops for a second and the two goons look at me blankly.

"I'M THE PRESIDENT OF LOOKOUT RECORDS."

Silence.

"YOU KNOW??? YA LIKE LOOKOUT RECORDS??? YA LIKE HARLEYS??? I GOTTA HARLEY!!!"

They leave the room. Mission accomplished.

The crowd is filing in. I walk over to the balcony and glance down at them. Not a pretty sight. I start to get slightly queasy thinking that there will soon be over five thousand people packed inside this room. I don't care much for crowds. I go back to the dressing room and begin a game of cribbage with Chris. After giving him a sound thrashing, I chew down a Xanax; there's only about 30 minutes until Jawbreaker hits the stage and what started out as a joke has turned into a reality — I am to introduce Jawbreaker tonight.

To get myself up for it, I pull out my little tape recorder and begin making idiotic notes to myself, occasionally interviewing anyone who comes my way. I walk out onto the side balcony and watch the people waiting for the El. I notice a crew member at the other end of the balcony so I approach him, tape running.

"How does the crowd look tonight?" I ask, thrusting the recorder in his face. "Ugly?"

"Oh yeah, very," he says. "They haven't improved."

"Do they frighten you as they frighten me?"

He gives a nervous laugh. "They terrify me."

I'm out of questions but I've never let that stop me before.

"Do you ever worry that England will declare war on you?"

"No," he answers thoughtfully. "They know that most of the income in the U.K. comes from Scotland. They'd never do that."

I'm a bit dejected. No dirt, no scoops, no nothing.

I head downstairs to the stage, where Bill is putting out the set lists. The crowd is cheering him. I walk onstage to ask him if I have time to hand out some copies of Panic Button. He tells me I have fifteen minutes. I go back upstairs, flashing my nifty pass at the security guards, grab the fanzines and head back out to the crowd. I have 100 copies with me. They're gone in about three minutes. One girl doesn't seem to want to take a copy.

"What is it?" she asks suspiciously.

"It's a fanzine."

Nothing.

"Punk rock."

Plenty of vacancies in this motel.

"IT'S FREE!"

"Awesome!" she says, grabbing for it.

Looking around, it hits me that the room is almost filled to capacity. I finish handing out the fanzines as little waves of dizziness hit me every few seconds. I start to head for the stairs and the safety of the dressing room when I run into Vapid and his girlfriend, who are standing around sipping beers, unable to get upstairs due to the status of their passes. The security squad has informed them that they'll be allowed behind the lines IF accompanied by someone with a higher level pass and only AFTER the dinner table has been cleared. Wouldn't want 'em eating that dumpster-bound food, would we?

We're discussing the ridiculousness of the scenario when a security guard lumbers over; he's spotted my tape recorder.

"Can I help you?" he asks.

"No," I say, smiling away like crazy.

"I'll need to take that," he replies, matching my smile. "I'll put it in the office and you can get it after the show."

I go into a long explanation about the recorder, lying my ass off about being a member of the press and having special permission from Jeff to carry the thing around. I know these mooks. They don't have the balls to go to Jeff with such petty shit. The ape goes over to the bottom of the stairs and consults a female security guard. They both walk back toward me, determination etched in their previously blank faces. Just as I'm about to receive a tongue-lashing and possibly have my recorder forcibly removed, a passerby accidentally bumps into me. My jacket slides open a little further, revealing my VIP pass. Their expressions immediately change.

"You're OK. I didn't see that," says my friend the security guard, pointing at my pass. "I'm just doing my job, y'know."

Yeah, I know.

I amble back toward the stairs, flash my pass and am halfway up when I spot a snotty looking collegiate-hippie type. I flip the recorder on.

"Excuse me," I say, making sure my pass is showing. "I'm doing a piece for *Rolling Stone*. Why are you here?"

The college boy looks at me blankly. I grab the pass and waggle it around furiously.

"Whattya think this is, buddy? Ya think they just GIVE these out??? WHO ARE YOU HERE TO SEE????"

My mock indignation has fanned whatever small fame of wit flickers inside his puny brain.

"I'm here to see both Mudhoney AND Nirvana."

"What about Jawbreaker?"

"I've never heard of them."

"Oh," I say, successfully concealing my disgust. "You're in for a treat."

Hippie boy moves on, but a gaggle of teenage boys who look like they just smoked their first joint has overheard. One of them asks how much I had to pay for the pass.

"I DID NOT PAY FOR THIS!" I say into the recorder. "I AM PAID TO DO THIS!!!"

"Oh," he says.

"I'm with *Hit Parader* magazine," I say, calming down a bit.

Seeing that the recorder is going, he uses this chance to express his individuality.

"My name is Chris and uh, therefore I am."

Huh???

His buddy jumps in.

"Hi, I'm Justin and all your music's great 'cause... I'm one of your biggest fans."

"What music is that?"

"Uh, Nirvana..."

"Okay."

"If there wasn't us," he continues, "there would be no you."

Hoo boy.

"That's true," I say agreeably. "You know, I think you boys have a lot of potential."

Their third pal, who's been standing back, suddenly grows balls.

"CENSORSHIP SUCKS!!!"

Good God! How to respond?

"Oh yeah," I say firmly. "Censorship does suck."

"Fuck censorship," he says, this time more quietly, as if pouting over the unfair fact that mom's just grounded him for a week.

"Damn right. FUCK CENSORSHIP!!!"

The boys cheer and I move on, impressed with the quality of human that will determine the course of the future of our nation.

I hop onto the stage to ask how much time I have before my introduction. Bill informs me that I have to do it NOW. Oh shit. I have no idea what I'm going to say. I have to say something besides "Here's Jawbreaker." But I am not a spoken word artist. I am not much of an ad-libber. I wish my bowels didn't feel like they'd just crumbled into a wet mush.

Jawbreaker is ready to go. They look at me.

I walk over to the center stage mike and am immediately greeted by the room-shaking roar of an impatient five-thousand-headed monster. I'm aware of a vague but nagging feeling that the recorder is running inside my zipped jacket pocket.

"Good evening."

(MASSIVE AUDIENCE ROAR. MY VOICE IS LOUDER THAN IT'S EVER BEEN OR EVER WILL BE)

"You don't even know who I am!"

(MORE MASS HYSTERIA. DO THEY EVEN UNDERSTAND THE WORDS I'M SPEAKING???)

"Let me introduce to you a fine young trio from San Francisco."

(SCREAMS, CHEERS)

"They've worked hard for years and years..."

(MORE SCREAMS — AN AUDIENCE MEMBER UP FRONT YELLS AN OBSCENITY AT ME)

"Didn't your mother ever teach you any manners?" I say, looking straight at him. He laughs. The massive beast rears its ugly head yet again.

"These young men play punk rock, a concept most of you are unfamiliar with."

(THE AUDIENCE REACTION SUGGESTS THAT THEY EITHER THINK I'M MOSES OR ELSE THEY DON'T KNOW OR CARE WHAT I'M SAYING. BANSHEES, SCREAMING, SCRATCHING BANSHEES, EVERY ONE OF THEM)

"They've slept with dogs. They've slogged through shit. They've gone through hell just to come here and entertain you at eighteen dollars a head."

(THE SALIVATING MONSTER SEEMS ON THE VERGE OF EXPLODING. HALF-PANICKED, I WONDER WHAT WOULD HAPPEN IF I ACTUALLY SAID SOMETHING OF SUBSTANCE. NO TIME FOR THAT...)

"All I can say is..."

(I CAN'T THINK OF ANYTHING TO SAY. NO, NOT THIS! I CAN'T GO LIMP NOW! JESUS CHRIST, I FEEL A GODDAMN RIOT COMING ON! THINK THINK THINK!!!)

I speak the first three words that pop into my befuddled head.

"Christ you're stupid."

Jawbreaker kicks in and I hide behind Blake's speaker cabinet with Bill. I'm actually trembling.

Back in the dressing room I ask Vapid to rate my introduction on a scale of 1 to 10. Before he can answer, Chris pipes up.

"You called them stupid punks."

"No I didn't. I said THIS is punk and I told 'em they were stupid for paying eighteen bucks a head."

"You said punk is stupid," says Bill.

"I thought it was great," says Vapid. "I give it an eight."

"Well," says Adam dryly, "if you had said the band's name you might've gained a couple more points..."

A young longhaired guy wearing a t-shirt featuring a mutation of the Black Flag logo walks in carrying The Baby — the infamous product of Cobain's loins. He's the nanny. Wait! It's the guy on the VIP pass! I sense a potential scoop. He's quite friendly and I'm pleased to discover that he's familiar with both my band and my writing.

He seems comfortable enough in my presence. I ask him how he got the job.

"I got the offer and I turned it down," he says. "Then three months later I still didn't have any money so I just called 'em and said okay."

"What qualified you for this position?"

"I'm trusted..." he stops for a moment while the baby lets out a particularly piercing scream. "I'm trusted in that camp. I have no baby experience. I turned twenty the day I started doing this."

"HOW old are you?"

He repeats himself. I heard him right the first time.

Pat Smear, ex-Germ and current Nirvana rhythm guitarist, has entered with a Heineken in his hand. He makes himself at home, joking with everyone in the room. He's an instant hit — a zany, if somewhat elderly, punk with a knack for the snappy comeback. I think I may be onto something here. I approach the matter delicately.

"How did Pat get on the tour?" I ask the nanny.

"I was playing the Australian (Germs) bootleg, what is that on, Ghost of Darb Records? And (Cobain) shouted it out. 'PAT! I'll call Pat!'"

"Come on. Did you get him on the tour?"

The nanny answers very quietly.

"Yes."

I realize that things aren't going to get any better for me than they are at this point. I have my scoop: THE NANNY IS RUNNING THE SHOW. The nanny leaves the baby with Pat while he heads out to the balcony with

43

Blake to catch up on old times and Bay Area happenings. Pat and I verbally spar as he attempts to hang on to both the baby and the Heineken. He's an unpretentious guy — quick-witted and somehow out of place on this tour. After he jokingly complains that there are no M&M's in the Nirvana dressing room, Bill and I quietly hatch a plan to give him all the fucking M&M's he could possibly want at an appropriate time.

"Are you a permanent member of the band?" I ask politely.

"I don't know," he says. "It's never been discussed."

I can't tell if he's kidding or not. I mean, he is living with the Cobain family in Seattle. It never came up???

Whether or not he's a permanent member, he undoubtedly brings punk rock credibility to the tour. He insists that no one in the crowd knows who he is. They probably don't, but the critics sure do.

When the nanny comes back I inform him of my angle. He seems to get a kick out of it. Pat remarks that the nanny is the sole reason Jawbreaker is on the tour. I ask if this is true. He hesitates for a few moments. Finally he speaks.

"Ummm... yeah."

More punk rock credibility, and it's all engineered quite innocently by a punk rock kid who's not even old enough to legally drink a beer.

My theory confirmed, I'm basically satisfied, though I'd sure like to get a peek in Nirvana's dressing room. Mudhoney is busy assaulting the crowd with their brand of early 1970's hard rock and Smear has left, presumably on a quest for more Heineken.

The nanny is more than happy to help me run the gauntlet to the main dressing room. A large crowd follows him from the Jawbreaker room to Nirvana's headquarters. I head over to Smear, who's sitting on a window ledge. While we politely insult each other, unbeknownst to me, those members of our group with the less-important passes are asked by a security guard, "Can I help you?" and quickly ushered out.

There isn't much happening in the Nirvana dressing room. A huge bowl of fruit sits on the bar along with a wide selection of sodas and bottled water. The proprietors of Shangri-La in my old neighborhood — Roscoe Village — sit alone on one of the white pleather couches that looks to have been swiped from Graceland. They must know somebody or they would've been kicked out by now.

I head into the bathroom to take a whizz. It's roomy, and unlike the communal public-style bathroom shared by the opening bands and the crew, it has a fairly clean, modern shower. But the toilet is lopsided and cracked and it looks like the room hasn't been mopped in a year. I realize that despite the enormity of this event, it still ain't the Lyric Opera.

Upon re-entering the room I catch a glimpse of Nirvana's drummer heading out the door. The Nirvana bassist, Chris, is talking with Smear. I approach them with a copy of Panic Button, which Smear has already refused to look at, citing an aversion to "corporate bullshit." Smear, apparently, is always on.

Chris leafs through my mag and comments on the nice layout.

"I'm sick of photocopied 'zines," he says. "Everybody's doing it."

He asks for a copy to read and then introduces himself. At the same moment, Cobain enters the room and stares me down for a second. I get the distinct feeling that he knows who I am and a slight shudder passes through me as I envision myself being beaten in an alley by members of the JAM security staff.

I break eye contact and concentrate on Chris, pointing out the fact that although he's only three years older than me, he makes at least 75 times as much money. I may have hit a sore spot.

"Can we have a big discussion on materialism and the accumulation of wealth?" he asks sarcastically. "It's all part of this consumer society..."

I hand him the recorder so he can continue his diatribe.

"I think this system here, this transaction-based, capitalist-type, market economy..."

I break in.

"You gonna be playing the hits tonight, like 'Jeremy'?"

He gives me back the recorder and allows Smear to field the question.

"Oh yeah," he says, "all the hits — 'Jeremy', 'Evenflow'..."

The baby has been crawling around the dressing room and now Cobain picks her up and takes her towards the open window, which is three stories up. He pretends to toss her out the window several times while singing loudly, "Would you kno-o-ow my na-a-ame..."

I interrupt.

"Hi, I'm Ben."

"Hi Ben."

"I'm just looking for a scoop."

"A scoo-oop."

Smear again intervenes.

"You're barking up the wrong tree," he tells me.

I'm fully aware that there's a paranoid attitude in the Nirvana camp these days regarding the press. Earlier in the week, someone from *USA*

Today had written something negative about the band and was flatly denied entrance to the subsequent show. Tonight it was rumored that absolutely no press people were to be allowed backstage. Obviously, no one was taking me very seriously as a press man because the Nirvana entourage didn't once question me about my recorder, which by this point I was directing at people like a machine gun.

The baby reaches out for the recorder and Cobain encourages her. "Throw it out the window," he says in his best talking-to-baby voice.

Cobain looks and speaks as if he's wacked out on smack. Having been in the presence of a few junkies in my time, I try to size up the situation and end up drawing a blank. The greasy hair, the nine days' growth, the putrid, ragged sweater he's wearing, the Jeff Spicoli vocal inflections — I can't figure out if it's an act or not.

He puts the baby down and — for some reason — gives me his full attention.

"Ben," he says. "Ben Weasel." He sounds as if he's greeting a long-lost friend.

"Mmmm, no," I answer. "Well, yeah, yes."

"Katie Smellie. Katy Odell."

"Are you an avid reader of *MaximumRockNRoll*?" I ask, seeing as how he's familiar with at least one of the other columnists.

"Avid," he answers. "The word 'avid.'"

"Do you read it a lot?"

"I used to." Now it appears he's going to take me somewhat seriously. "Y'know, I kinda forgot it existed for a long time but every once in a while, yeah, I look through it."

"Do you like it?"

"I think... ummm... I'm really happy about the fact that it will decompose within about ten years."

I make a comment about that very scenario being MRR editor Tim Yohannan's apparent goal, seeing as how he doesn't save the originals for any of the issues.

Cobain is now getting a little worked up.

"I can't have a comment on *MaximumRockNRoll*, fuck that. I mean, those people hate our guts. I would hate our guts too if I was a fifteen-year-old kid who only listened to... or who only read *MaximumRockNRoll* and only listened to punk rock bands."

"Were you ever that?"

"Yeah."

"And you felt that way?"

"Exactly. I was just as closed-minded as those people."

I consider enlightening him about the fact that almost half the staff at MRR was writing about how great Nirvana was when Nevermind came out, but then I realize that like so many other stars, this guy only reads the bad press. I'm more than a little shocked that he has such an obvious hatred for a magazine — a fanzine, really — which doesn't mean shit in his world. Somehow, someway, MRR's validation of his efforts (or lack thereof) matters. This amazes me.

The bass player interrupts our little session by informing the band that they have to go on stage.

We leave the dressing room and I reflect on Cobain's statements and demeanor. The whole thing strikes me as being a little odd.

I've been told that the heroin problems he and his wife have had were made public knowledge by one of his own "people" (in fact, the guy rumored to be responsible worked with Tim Yohannan on MRR radio back in the old days). True or not, it comes across as manufactured. I ponder Cobain's appearance and style of speaking and still have trouble deciding whether he's a perpetually stoned, developmentally arrested rock star or a fuck-up like the rest of us who's scared to death of all the hype and publicity surrounding his band. It's obviously all thrown the guy into another world. His band mates appear to be comfortable and at peace with their situation; Cobain is still begging the teacher for another five minutes to finish the test.

Just before Bill and I near the ramp at stage left, we witness a shirtless kid, obviously fucked up out of his mind, being tossed out by JAM security. Nirvana is still in the middle of their first song. The kid is pleading with the bouncers to let him stay. He pulls out a wad of bills and starts counting, 20, 40, 60, 80, 100. The security guys are chuckling. They take his money and he's allowed back in.

When Bill and I reach the stage, we settle in off to the side, out of sight of the audience. We immediately grab the M&M's from our pockets and begin whipping them at Smear, who plays along by attempting to catch them in his mouth while at the same time cranking out the hit single from the new Nirvana album.

Kurt Cobain is in another world. The rest of the band is jamming, occasionally smiling, having a good time. Not once do I see Cobain make eye contact with his band mates, let alone acknowledge their presence. The band is tight, but there are long, uncomfortable spaces between songs. Cobain takes his sweet time, often heading over to the rack of over a dozen custom-made left handed guitars to change instruments. The bassist tries to make some wisecracks to the crowd and Cobain is not pleased. The crowd is oblivious; the band could do Dead Milkmen covers at this point and no one would mind.

Bill and I decide to bail out from our stage left position after a few songs; nothing's happening here and every time the band starts a new tune I could swear it was the one they just played. As we turn to leave the stage, two kids run up the ramp and barrel past us, diving into the crowd from the stage just like they've seen on MTV. When Bill and I open the backstage doors, we see that the offending stage divers are in the clutches of two large JAM security men who seem quite close to beating the living shit out of them; one of the kids landed on a fellow security man's head.

The JAM guys turn and see us and seem prepared to kick us out. Once they see our passes, they attempt to bring us into their nasty little circle. They're both shouting a lecture-style denouncement of stage diving at the kids, pointing out the possible damage they could cause to people. They occasionally look over at us as if we're supposed to nod in agreement, if not join in. We're both silent, simply watching out to make sure the kids don't end up in the hospital. Finally, the offended security guard walks in and is asked if he wants to press charges.

"Goddamn right," he answers.

The kids, enjoying the effects of some kind of illicit drug or another, seem to have little idea of what's going on, and as they're led back through the crowd to be handed over to the cops, I get the feeling that they think they're being let back into the show.

At the end of Nirvana's set, the crowd is pissed off. Their heroes have refused to play "Smells Like Teen Spirit." Cobain reacts by diving off the stage into the crowd and promptly loses his shoes. No security guards threaten to have him arrested.

As the crowd piles onto the street, Bill and Blake stand in front of the venue hawking t-shirts and CD's; to sell them inside would've meant that everything would've been priced at an obscene level. A cop attempts to harass Blake about selling the shirts. Blake waves him off, telling him he's in the band.

"Okay," says the cop, "but don't be a smart ass with me. I can still haul you in to jail."

The t-shirts are going like crazy. I get the feeling these cretins would buy fresh dog shit if there was a flashy sign on it. From deep in the crowd,

I hear a loud scream. I can't make out the words. A minute later, I hear it again, this time closer and clear as a bell.
"LEGALIZE IT!!!"
For a brief moment, I hope he's talking about murder.

Before we head back to my apartment, Bill and Vapid plaster a couple of Screeching Weasel stickers on the backs of the Wave Dancer and the Blue Mirage. The evening has been a success.

A few days later, Jim DeRogatis from the *Sun-Times* informs me that Cobain's junkie appearance that night was probably due to the fact that he'd taken a sleeping pill earlier in the day. Still, I'm not surprised when, two months later, I see him on MTV Unplugged wearing the same ratty sweater, sporting the same greasy hair and nine days' growth and looking slightly spacey. Smear is still with the band, quiet and unobtrusive, playing his guitar off to the left of the stage.

The next Friday, Screeching Weasel plays in Janesville, Wisconsin. The promoter had attended the Nirvana show in Milwaukee that took place the night after their Chicago gig. He'd met up with Blake, who'd given him a present to pass on to me. The promoter hands me a pack of Kools. Written on them in black marker is a message from Blake: SMOKE 'EM IF YOU GOT 'EM.
Yes.

MAXIMUM STYLE

PART ONE: SHUT UP AND EAT!
The photo heading this column depicts yours truly munching down on a hat. Though I don't remember saying so, Ramsey from AK Press tells me that I once swore I'd eat my hat if Jawbreaker signed to a major label. Like I said, I don't remember uttering such an oath but it sure as fuck SOUNDS like something I'd say and Ramsey has no reason to lie to me (other than to laugh at me while I eat my hat). Jawbreaker still haven't officially signed yet but the hat has been eaten, the fat lady has sung, the show is fucking over.

"JAWBREAKER WILL NEVER SIGN TO A MAJOR LABEL." When Blake told me that, I asked him to repeat it loudly into the tape recorder so I could have it for the record. When everybody was giving them shit for selling out even though they hadn't sold a thing and didn't plan to, I stood behind them one hundred fucking percent. They made me look stupid, and for that I'm kinda pissed. But Blake, Chris and Adam are my friends so I have to cut 'em some slack. And truthfully, I'm more disappointed than pissed. They coulda done it their way. They coulda been the biggest indie band EVER. They coulda talked the talk and walked the walk. It sucks. It's probably going to mean their band will end a lot quicker than it should. But in this case, I have to separate business and friendship and no matter how stupid I think this move is, they're still great guys and they're still a great band.

As a fan of Jawbreaker, you have the right to be pissed as well. They know it and I think they're prepared to take all the shit that's gonna be flung their way because they're men, not mice. But I don't think I'll ever again believe a band that tells me they won't sell, even though they probably mean it, as Jawbreaker did at the time.

Either way, the hat is digesting.

PART TWO: YOU LOOK LIKE A DORK

In the past three months, MRR's circulation has doubled. (*Editor's note: This is a fine example of our columnists' literary license — the reality is that our circulation does go up slowly but steadily, about 500 copies a month*). Because of this, a lot of you yo-yo's reading this column are newcomers and probably not aware of my feelings about the current fashion trends in punk rock. Even the people who HAVE been reading my column like good little doobies apparently haven't been taking me seriously because they're still dressing like complete and total dorks.

I suggest you pay close attention to what I'm about to tell you because it could very well change your life. Without any further hoopla, I present THE OFFICIAL PUNK ROCK DRESS CODE.

1. Baseball caps are nice. I own a total of five baseball caps myself and I often wear my Cubs cap or my USA: AMERICAN AND PROUD cap when I go out to pick up the mail or stock up on Gatorade for the weekend. But I would no more wear a ball cap to a gig than I would a fez. Ball caps have no fucking place in punk rock (though the sport of baseball itself has a very important place in punk rock — I'll get to that some other time). So from here on in, anyone who wears a ball cap to a gig is a fucking jerk.

2. Baggy shorts have no place in punk rock. Baggy shorts are a product of the hip hop scene and it's there they should remain. Nobody wants to see your turd-crusted butt crack and your piss-stained skivvies. Nobody is impressed by that stupid goddamn chain on your wallet hanging down five feet like a pair of mittens your mother clipped to your parka. If you forget to bring this column with you to your next gig after you've clipped it neatly from these pages, just remember this: Baggy pants = DORK. NO EXCEPTIONS! (I also have strong feelings about baggy t-shirts. Baggy t-shirts wearers, however, are NOT necessarily dorks, because often times they have no choice in the matter; too many bands have succumbed to the pressure to only stock XL t-shirts in their vans, thus ensuring that the well-meaning punks will end up LOOKING like dorks. FUCK any band who doesn't sell LARGE t-shirts as well as [or better yet, instead of] XL t-shirts.)

3. Backpacks. Backpacks are for school or hiking trips. They are not for gigs. Punk rock shows do not generally take place in the uncharted wilderness; there is no need for a backpack. They are aesthetically unpleasing, but worse, there is no PRACTICAL reason for wearing a backpack to a show; anything that can't fit into the pockets of your leather jacket is most likely unnecessary anyway. Which brings me to the most important segment of the PUNK ROCK DRESS CODE: what you SHOULD wear.

First of all and most important is this: If you think you're a punk and you don't own a leather jacket, you're not a punk. The whiniest of you are thinking to yourselves, WELL I DON'T CARE. I DON'T WANNA BE CLASSIFIED AS A PUNK ANYWAY. Shut up and go home. Real punks wear real leather jackets. Real punks wear real leather jackets WITHOUT stupid spikes or studs or patches or paintings or stickers or band names plastered all over them. If you're a punk, your leather jacket is adorned only by a few tastefully placed buttons on the lapels. Since we have to take differing climates into account, you can't be expected to wear a leather jacket EVERY time you go to a gig. But if you don't wear your leather jacket at least 65% of the time when you go out, you're no punk.

Secondly, footwear is more important than you may think. If you wear Doc Martens, you're not a punk. If you wear Doc Martens, you're a sucker. ANY other kind of boot is acceptable. As far as sneakers go, there is one and only one acceptable brand and that is Chuck Taylor Converse All-Star hi-tops. Now I know you already know that, but what you don't know is that punks DO NOT wear red converse, Christmas Converse, plaid Converse or any kind of Converse except for black. Uh, that is until recently. After communicating with Stevie of the now-defunct Devil Dogs AND learning that Samiam gets paid to wear black Converse at least 50% of their onstage time, I've come to the realization that black C.T.'s have been co-opted by the mainstream and are now completely unacceptable. I KNOW what you're thinking. You're thinking, BUT, BUT, BUT ALL SORTS OF MAINSTREAM PEOPLE WEAR LEATHER JACKETS AND YOU SAID LEATHER JACKETS ARE THE NUMBER ONE PRIORITY OF THE PUNK ROCK DRESS CODE. Fuck you, I know what I said. The point is, leather jackets are not a SYMBOL of MAINSTREAM ALTERNATIVE/ PUNK. Black C.T.'s ARE.

Because this is such a recent development, there will be a grace period of three months from the publication of this column during which you will not be considered a total fucking twit if spotted sporting black C.T.'s. But after that three months, your C.T.'s should be white. No other colors, no funky laces or writing on the shoes, just plain white. Don't even try to argue about it because I've gone over every argument in my own head. There is no other way.

You already know that baggy pants are for the birds. Aside from that, there's a decent amount of leeway in the PUNK ROCK DRESS CODE as far as pants go, though you're really better off sticking with blue or black jeans (LEVI'S ONLY! NO GAP, WRANGLER, TOUGHSKINS, JORDACHE, SERGIO or whatever the fuck else you might find).

And though you can wear just about any jacket during the 35% of the time when you're not sporting your nifty leather, UNDER NO CIRCUMSTANCES should a punk be seen wearing a gas station jacket. Gas station jackets are for pussies. Gas station jackets are for guys with 20/20 vision who wear glasses anyway to impress the dimwitted emo chicks. The gas station jacket is the '90s version of the Nehru jacket and years from now, when you idiots look back at photos of yourselves in 1995 because your snot-nosed kids asked you if you ever did anything besides selling insurance, you will cringe.

That's it. For the one dumb fucker in Hungary who's sharpening up his angry-letter pencil at this very moment, lighten up. My PUNK ROCK DRESS CODE is only wishful thinking (though those of you who adhere to it will thank me later).

And lemme tell you something else about punks, punk. IF YOU DON'T THINK THE RAMONES WERE THE GREATEST BAND TO EVER WALK THE EARTH, YOU ARE NOT A PUNK. YOU ARE NOT EVEN FUCKING CLOSE. YOU HAVE NO BUSINESS BEING IN A BAND, DOING A FANZINE OR SHOWING YOUR SORRY FACE AT A GIG. IF YOU PLACE ANY BAND ABOVE THE RAMONES, YOU ARE AN IDIOT. I WILL BE BUYING INSURANCE FROM YOU COME JULY.

PUNK IS A FOUR-LETTER WORD

One of the few things I'm proud of from 1986-1988 was that in every ad Screeching Weasel took out, in every interview we gave and on every record we released, we not only didn't shy away from the word "punk," we embraced it. Why wouldn't we? It described the type of music we were playing. It still does. I've never felt comfortable with the label "pop-punk." I guess I don't like it because it puts the "pop" before the "punk." We have never, in my ever-humble opinion, released a record that was a pop record filtered through a punk sensibility. Our records have always been punk records with a nod (and maybe even a handshake) to good pop music (and also to good heavy metal music, but that's a whole different subject...).

It's not a bad thing to acknowledge that punk rock is a type of music defined by its stylistic differences from regular old rock and roll. And maybe it's not such a bad thing for somebody to call him or herself a punk. It means something to them. A couple of years ago, I would've laughed at anybody who called themselves a punk, but with the rise of consumerism and the decline of purpose in the punk scene, I'm more than willing to afford a little respect to somebody who stands for something, as much as I may not be willing to take on the same label.

Most of you people don't stand for anything. I'd rather hang around somebody with a bunch of crackpot beliefs than yet another smart-ass kid who has the same bullshit, sitcom belief system that I kissed goodbye in 1983. You know, I guess there's nothing wrong with being a college student, but exactly when the fuck did that shit become the slightest bit important? What happened to the concept that punks were world-class fuck-ups? I'm not talking about drunken, violent idiots, or the Postcard Punks who you used to find on Clark and Belmont in Chicago, or on Telegraph in Berkeley or on Queen Street in Toronto, the ones who would charge tourists a few bucks to take their photo ("...and there's George in front of the Dunkin' Donuts with a 'punk rocker.' His hairstyle is called a 'mohawk.'"), I'm talking about people who didn't fit in, not because they didn't want to but because they couldn't. And then, because they couldn't, they didn't want to, and they gave the one-finger salute to society and created their own thing with a sense of purpose and conviction that the hippies gave up in favor of listening to Billy Joel and Toto and living a 2.3 children lifestyle. Listen up, dumb ass: An entire fucking scene — the one that enables you to see Rancid on MTV in 1997 — was created by a bunch of maniacal fucking misfits. Those same misfits, fuck-ups and losers nurtured that scene and helped new people who came along and wanted to be a part of something different. They made that scene thrive, and it grew into the monster that it is today. (And I think it's funny as hell that people take shots at guys like Tim Yohannan, who's been sticking by his beliefs since he started publishing *Maximum RockNRoll* in 1981. People claim that Tim has "changed," when in reality, all Tim is guilty of is exactly the opposite: NOT changing. The fine line between having the strength of your convictions and becoming a living dinosaur is actually a pretty clear line to me, so I'll refrain from getting into it this time around. Maybe next time. Somebody remind me...)

  It's so cute when you all debate about a band's decision to sell out their fans so they can sell more records, but you forget that the reason those bands have the opportunity to make that decision is because for the longest time, we didn't care about selling records to the mainstream and so we didn't try; we were too busy making the music that eventually would come into favor with the mainstream.

  So many of you are so proud to say you're not punks. Well, when Screeching Weasel started out nobody wanted to say they were a punk, either. "I don't want to be categorized." "Don't pigeonhole me." Fuck you, kiddo. I'll put your fucking head in a milk bottle (©19something — Angry Samoans), you dirty cocksucker. I mean, I don't seriously believe that we should all turn into a bunch of zombies and wander around with mohawks bumping into shit like the Postcard Punks used to do. But goddamnit, there was a time when you knew who was the fucking enemy, and part of the reason that those lines have shifted around so much is because everybody's too goddamned scared to stand up and say what they believe in, and really believe it, enough to take a punch in the mouth if it comes to it. The punk scene is, more than ever, filled with a bunch of would-be intellectuals who want to discuss everything to death. It's the Bay Area (of Northern California) syndrome: "Somebody's upset about something? Let's have a meeting!" I'm tired of fucking meetings. I'm tired of taking seriously people who are a fucking joke. I'm tired of listening to people who oughta just shut the fuck up.

Now, when people start calling themselves punks, this creates a whole new set of problems. They create stringent rules, usually with good intentions, but rules that nonetheless end up driving people away. They fall prey to a mindless provincialism that makes one want to smash some bottles on some heads. No, no, no — "punk rockers" are a whole different can of worms. But despite that, I still can't help but feel anything but contempt for those of you twits who don't have the guts to believe in anything, let alone to stand up for those beliefs. At least if you called yourself a punk I'd have a ballpark idea of where you stood.

And that leads me to what I'm really sick of, which is the de-politicization of punk. I spent a lot of years — and I don't regret it for a second — railing against the politically correct. This was before the term "politically correct" entered the mainstream, and before the right adopted it. Contrary to the usual hip-liberal propaganda masters' theories of its origins, "politically correct" was a term coined by the left to describe the lunatic fringe amongst itself. It was a term you could find in any punk fanzine in the early and mid-eighties. It only entered the mainstream in the nineties (and rightfully so), when political correctness on college campuses and in the workplace reached totalitarian proportions. Rape was re-defined to include — in some cases — literally looking at someone the wrong way. Anybody who didn't toe the line was a sexist, or a racist. Asinine terms like "Native American" and "African-American" began popping up. (Nobody asked the Indians or blacks if they approved of these terms. A Gallup poll from 1994 indicates they didn't. American Indians were asked what they wanted to be called. Their answers, in order of preference, were 1. Indians, 2. Don't care, 3. Native Americans. The percentages for "Native Americans" were substantially lower than they were for "Don't care." Similarly, "African-American" came in third behind "Don't care" and "Black" among blacks. That said, polls must be taken with a grain of salt. And that said, those terms were thought up not by blacks or Indians, but by guilty white liberals).

I hated political correctness and I fought it tooth and nail as it reared its ugly head in the punk scene. I'm glad I did. But now, it seems that everyone's become completely de-politicized. That's partially due to the

P.C. backlash, but it's also due in no small part to the shift in the punk scene from social politics (as opposed to "political politics" — social politics is the first Dead Kennedys record. Political politics is Jello Biafra's spoken word records) to consumerism. Believe it or not, there was a time when most punk bands were politically aware. These bands, all of which descended from the original post-punk bands of the late seventies and early eighties, were politically aware because it was the norm. People in the punk scene did not, by and large, buy into the easy chair, sitcom mentality that the rest of the country so readily accepts. Punk bands, and fanzine writers, and people who booked shows, and fans, were, by and large, aware that this country is run by a wealthy, white power structure who just loves watching black against white, male against female, straight against gay, because it lets them line their pockets without ever being questioned. Poor to middle-class whites are busy blaming lazy spics and niggers for unemployment? Good! They're not going to have time to figure out that the real problem is that the chairman of the board gave himself and his cronies a raise of a few million bucks a year. Why sacrifice your raise when you can just close a few factories?

This stuff was commonly known. I don't think it is any longer. I like to just turn off my brain and crank up the music like anybody else. I don't like being subjected to boring, heavy-handed lectures. But in the past, there were always at least a few political bands that had creative and highly entertaining ways of politicizing their music. The Dead Kennedys did it on their first record. Born Against did it — and they did it particularly well at the end of their existence as a band. Moral Crux still does it pretty damn well. But by and large, wicked, vicious little jabs at society-at-large (as well as the punk scene — the microcosm of society that we turn to for our musical entertainment), are a thing of the past. And that's not good.

The world is a more fucked up place than ever. Racism, sexism, and anti-gay sentiments are still running rampant. And the consumer-driven mindlessness that fuels those sentiments is firmly entrenched in the punk scene. That's why there are still a few well meaning, if wildly misguided, people running around screaming "SELL-OUT!" Fucking shit, at least they're screaming something. And if you — those of you who look down your nose at those people (and I'll include myself in that group) — don't offer a more intelligent, reasoned viewpoint, then you're just a sucker, and as far as I'm concerned, you haven't earned the right to say a fucking word about it. I believe that it's your responsibility as a human being to do what's right and to develop your beliefs based on a code of common decency. If you don't want to, don't. But don't get in my way, 'cause I'll run you the fuck down, chump.

MAXIMUM STYLE REVISITED

First — and I noticed a few of these Web site messages last month but simply forgot to comment on them — yet another poor, misguided child has gone astray and I've got the feeling that I could be blamed — that I could be pegged as some kind of Pied Piper of Punktown.

So listen up and listen good. A couple of years ago, I wrote a column for *MaximumRockNRoll* which primarily concerned a facetious "punk rock dress code." In the course of this mildly amusing mini-thesis, I described what was and wasn't proper attire for today's hip young punk rocker. The column was born of disgust at seeing how many punks had co-opted the hip hop look or else were dressing like any other kid on the street. The fact that I was in San Francisco (home of MRR) at the time, had no column to turn in and decided to prove to Tim Yohannan — the publisher of the article in question — that I could write, re-write and copyedit a column in twenty minutes also contributed greatly to the theme and tone of the column.

Though I made it clear in the column that I didn't expect anyone to take me seriously, some of you went ahead and did it anyway. I'm told that now, in addition to the chain wallet, baggy pants crowd, there's a zombie-like contingent of nitwits walking around in leather jackets, t-shirts, jeans and white Chuck Taylor All-Star high tops. Admittedly, I still dress this way myself. I've dressed this way since I was a teenager (if you change the type of sneakers and lose the leather jacket, I've been dressing this way since I was a child). I'm not very creative in the clothes department. The only things I look good in are the aforementioned items of clothing or suits. No kidding, I look pretty sharp in a good suit.

But back to the point. I haven't been out to see a punk show in several years. In fact, the last time I saw a punk band live was when the Riverdales played with the Mr. T Experience at the end of our tour just about two years ago. But were I to go out to a gig tomorrow night and have to suffer through the sight of a bunch of little me's, I think I might cringe myself into a permanent grimace. It would be weird enough to have to deal with running into people I haven't seen in years, but to have to do it while a bunch of cartoon copies of myself were hanging around would be unbearable.

Dress the way you want to dress. Please don't follow my punk rock dress code. I wrote it as a joke two years ago. It doesn't mean anything. It's not to be taken seriously. For the love of Pete, just cut it out. Please.

On a different note, regarding the people who wish we were "easier to see in concert," or who want to invite us to play their town where we can stay at their house and have a free meal, let me explain a couple of things to you.

One, we don't play concerts. We play shows. I like to call them gigs, but whatever they are, they are most definitely not concerts. There are a lot of reasons why our performances can't be termed concerts, but the most important two are that we don't stay on stage for an hour and we don't take requests.

Second, inviting us to stay at your house and eat pizza with you is not much of an inducement for us to play your town. For all I know, that's how all the other bands do it. But for us, when we started making money from music, we realized that A. It was kind of cheap for us to still be trying to sleep on people's floors for free and B. Nothing is really free. We got real tired real quick of being promised a quiet place to stay and instead being forced to listen to music, drunken and/or stoned idiots clamoring around trying to impress us by acting like they didn't notice us and moron "hosts" whose primary interest in having us stay at their home fell into one or both of the following categories:

A. "Hey, losers, guess who stayed at my house last night?"

B. "Hey, losers, guess what Danny from Screeching Weasel told me last night about Bobby Braindead from the Dumass Gerkoffs?"

In short, if we play your town, we'll be staying at a motel. Or maybe even a hotel. No matter where we stay, I can guarantee you that we won't be sleeping on your floor. But thanks for the offer.

And by the way, referring to us as "assholes" for not playing your town or demanding to know "why the fuck" we don't play your town, is a big part of the reason why we don't play your town. Didn't I explain that last month???

Well either way, I've got a church choir meeting to get to.

Until next time...

YOU DAMN KIDS WITH YOUR INTERNET
AND YOUR LOUD ROCK MUSIC!

Unbelievable. You have nothing to say. Not one morsel of wit. Not a nugget of intelligence. Not even the feeblest attempts to inject in the midst of so much garbage a shred of original thought that might possibly lead to enlightening — or at least entertaining — discourse. I can't possibly respond to such utter nonsense as has been posted on this Web site in the past month. To do so would be to degrade myself, to lower myself to the level of a leering, greasy pot-dealer cruising the high school parking lot in his van, trying to pick up girls half his age.

I understand now why people my age and much, much older spend so much time engaging in back-and-forths with you witless, clueless, brainless, gutless pinheads: it makes them feel smart. Engaging in discourse with someone of their own intelligence, experience, knowledge or command of the ins and outs of creative debating is simply too difficult for these socially retarded chuckleheads. My peers choose instead to take the easy way out; they put their Yugos into drive, get into the slow lane of the information superhighway and proceed to putt-putt their way to inanity via the moist and sticky globules of gunk that pass for your collective intellect. It's called fish in a barrel, dummies, and you're the fish, and to be honest with you, I have better things to do than to pull out my .357 and start plugging away at you guppies.

Say something intelligent, get a halfway accurate spelling of the words you're using, learn the basic rules of capitalization and punctuation and try to express yourself in a manner that doesn't make you sound like the dimwit who left the message just before you. Do these things, and we'll talk via the modern wonders of computer communications. Do these things and I'll be happy to play with you. Until then, you can keep on playing with yourselves.

Several friends and acquaintances who really ought to know better have been browbeating me for a few years now regarding my lack of an e-mail address.

I don't need an e-mail address, I tell these well-meaning but severely misguided souls, because I already rent a box at the post office, and I have a mailbox, two separate telephone lines and a fax machine in my apartment. Anyone who needs to get in touch with me can. Anyone who needs to get in touch with me pronto can as well, provided I want them to be able to do so. The people who matter have my telephone numbers and can call anytime anything urgent comes up. If they don't want to talk (and I understand — there are times when you'd just rather write a note), they can fax me 24 hours a day. If the fax machine is out of paper or otherwise malfunctioning, it will still save up to twenty pages in its memory.

So you see, there's no logical reason for me to have an e-mail address. In fact, the only reason for me to get an e-mail address would be if I wanted one, and I most decidedly don't.

I am so incredibly tired of the condensation of communication and information that I've been witnessing over the past five years. I am thoroughly fed up with having to swallow the reality that as technology evolves, it's used not to make life better — or at least easier — for the inhabitants of this planet, but rather to distance ourselves from each other even more than we already are. As far as I'm concerned, a conversation with a person — face to face — is still the best form of communication, both for informational purposes as well as for the joy of experiencing the art of conversation — and I truly believe it is an art.

A telephone conversation can serve the same purpose but not as adequately; it's missing a crucial element: being able to look into another person's eyes or to read their body language. We also tend to get more easily distracted on the phone; think of all the things we allow to intrude upon our attention while we're on the telephone that we would never allow in a face to face (call waiting is one such example). But the biggest difference in the level of telephone communication is the lack of ability to see the other person, to interact, making even pure information exchanging a more difficult process; I need my hands when I talk, and my face and my eyes and sometimes my whole body. (And when videophones infiltrate our culture and become affordable, I'll be the first in line to pick one up.)

The answering machine message is generally an ugly, offensive thing, unless used to quickly impart information that requires no analyzation, confirmation or further communication of any type or if it's used to simply say, "I'd like to speak with you. Please return my call." Personally, I enjoy leaving long, rambling messages on people's machines. I often tell stories that have no point. Sometimes I'll tell the unlucky recipient of my message about the dream I had last night, or what I had for breakfast or what the weather is like here in Chicago. I leave these messages with my tongue planted firmly in my cheek in the hopes that they provide a little entertainment for the people who receive them — that they may serve as a brief reprieve from their daily duties and that they may provide them with a mild chuckle.

The letter, while lacking certain components crucial to a quality conversation, is an art form unto itself. The purpose of writing a letter is essentially the same purpose of writing an article for a magazine, or a story or a book. Your job as a letter writer is to dramatize whatever it is you're writing about, whether it's the alligator attack you survived last week, the fact that your boyfriend dumped you or the ordeal you've gone through in having to try to make the cat swallow his pills (and it's funny, but people tend to write so passionately about their pets. I have a friend who is one of the great letter writers. A well-known punk rock celebrity, this man would be the last person you'd think to write about his dog. But I receive a letter from him at least twice a month and he never fails to tell me about the dog's latest exploits and I'm completely drawn in to the point where I feel like I know this dog. This from a guy who never went to college, who, as far as I know, didn't even finish high school, and who has never written anything you'd have read, even for a fanzine). The letter is not so much a form of give and take conversation as it is an artistic account of one's latest exploits, mundane as they may be.

The fax is, in my experience, used primarily for business. It imparts factual information. I offer you a list of every fax I received yesterday: a proposed agreement from Lookout Records (rejected), a request from a German friend to store some tape reels (which request was made more cheaply via fax than it could've been via telephone), samples of a design for a new Riverdales t-shirt from an artist in Canada, a request from a local record label for a phone number for a distributor, and your precious comments forwarded by the guy who does the Web site you're currently trudging through. The fax machine is a necessity in my life and has been ever since I discovered that it made everything in my business life move much faster.

But e-mail is a different monster. E-mail is to the art of conversation as a '70s porn loop of a woman fucking a German Shepherd is to the Mona Lisa. Through rapid-fire, stream-of-consciousness missives written in a style that can only be described as Moron Shorthand, e-mail reduces the varied and beautiful languages of the world to a series of grunts, much in the way our Neanderthal ancestors must have communicated. While I'm all for reducing certain things to their most basic elements — music and fucking are two that come immediately to mind — communication is not among them. The conversationalist tells an adversary that he is an uncouth cad unworthy of the speaker's respect; that he acts in ways befitting a drunken ape; and that he deserves to be flogged with the whips of intelligence until some insight and decency finally begin to seep through his pores. The e-mailer tells said adversary to fuck off and calls him an asshole. And spells "asshole" wrong.

E-mail is, by nature, an affront to the art of communication. As an alternative to a fax machine, I suppose it serves its purpose. But used as a back and forth communication tool, it has destroyed the communication skills of the Internet generation (or perhaps never allowed those skills to develop in the first place) to the point where original thoughts are verboten; to where the common courtesy of phrasing a sentence in a way that suggests some thought was put into it no longer matters; to where visual assaults upon the reader via the ignorance of capitalization, punctuation and grammar are commonplace; to where the art of communication — and maybe more importantly, the gift of language — are shat upon; to where wandering around the Internet scratching oneself whilst emitting written grunts, belches and farts is par for the course; and to where the most one can expect from the e-mailer is a use of language and communication that approaches that of the dialogue in the average Pepsi commercial.

Yeah, the schools suck, but parents and government officials complained about shitty schools when I was a kid. Yeah, people don't read enough — that's a big part of the problem — but have people ever read enough? Yeah, kids play too many video games and have too few real-life adventures. But virtual reality — and I really like that term because I think it's incredibly accurate in describing the state you enter the second you log onto the Internet — has for many of you become a substitute for reality. Your social skills have suffered accordingly and your communication skills have either failed to develop maturely or have deteriorated altogether. You have isolated yourselves further from the rest of society — strangely, though you may "talk" to more people on the Internet than you do in the rest of your life, you have fewer friends and less meaningful conversations.

There is no information superhighway. There's just a large Twinkie floating out there in cyberspace, millions of people attached to its fluffy, sponge-like outer shell, attempting to get to the creamy, unnaturally white chemical-filled inside like so many ants.

But you can do research on the Internet! It has so many practical applications! Indeed it does, but how many of you actually spend your time on the net exploring those avenues? Isn't most of your time actually spent engaging in the banal cyberspace activities that you so loudly decry when defending your precious virtual world? The Internet itself is not a problem for me — evolving technology never really is — but rather it's the way in which people choose to use it. The Internet may offer a lot of positive things, but for all intents and purposes, it's an inherently racist, classist, interactive television for white, suburban, upper middle class people. Your feeble assertions that poor people can access the Internet at their public libraries don't hold water; you're conveniently ignoring the fact that there ain't no libraries in crack central and that the black kids on the West Side of Chicago and the Latinos in East L.A. don't attend schools that are equipped with computers that get them on the net and that through a systematic racism unwittingly perpetuated by people exactly you, few of them will ever have the opportunity to attend a college — even a community college. They are not on the Internet and their schools and libraries aren't getting them on the Internet and they sure as hell don't have the kind of money or time that you safe, comfortable, spoiled little brats do to buy and update computers and to pay a monthly subscription fee to an ISP so they can sit around on their fat little butts all day calling each other names like you do.

This privatized, all-access (for those who can afford it) superhighway supposedly leads to information and subsequently knowledge, and we all know that knowledge is power. But even before the government started sticking its fat nose into it, most of you were already hooked up with one of the monolithic ISP's who bind you to an oath to not use language they deem offensive — you are, despite the cutting-edge technology involved, stuck in the 1950's at an all-white, midnight college bull session that's being monitored by Joe McCarthy, Carrie Nation and Miss Manners. You're not gaining knowledge or experience and you're sure as hell not cruising down some fucking mythic information superhighway; you're being taken for a ride down a dead end street in an Edsel.

I'm not anti-technology. I need my hopelessly outmoded computer to write, and to help me conduct my business. I'm happy as a clam with my stereo system and laserdisc player (and when DVD becomes affordable, I'll be there). Hell, I've been defending my own television watching for years. Technology is never the problem. It's people who are the problem. You are the problem. And if you ever want to climb out of the pit of ignorance in which you wallow so comfortably, the first step is to realize what you're dealing with. Stop kidding yourself. Know the Internet for what it is. *Écrasez l'infâme.*

I'm through attempting to communicate with you monthly. If any of you come up with anything interesting to say, I'll take the time to post something. In the meantime, there are porches to sit on, barbecues with the neighbors to enjoy, and long, pointless walks to take in which I might end up in the park at 2:00 A.M., where I can sit under the trees and look up at the sky. Oh, and as always, choir practice beckons.

EULOGY FOR A FRIEND

Most anyone who reads this will know by now that Tim Yohannan, publisher of *MaximumRockNRoll*, died about three weeks ago. April 3rd, to be exact. There's been a lot of talk about what a huge influence he had on punk rock. I can't argue with that; I simply wouldn't be doing what I'm doing today if it weren't for Tim.

I first read *MaximumRockNRoll* in 1984. That magazine and the Ramones have been two of the biggest influences on my life. When Screeching Weasel's demo tape was reviewed in MRR in the fall of 1986 by Tim Yo, I was fucking *thrilled*. Tim Yohannan, the godfather of punk, thought my band was good. For an eighteen-year old kid, it was a big deal. The next year, Tim answered the phone when I called to book us at the Gilman St. Warehouse (a place that, at the time, was an anti-club designed to completely change the conventional idea of what a punk venue was), and he treated me like a person, not a stupid kid. I didn't have to kiss his ass. We were a punk band, he was familiar with us, and that was enough for Tim. He booked us (we wouldn't actually make it out to Gilman until 1988). That year he also reviewed our first album, and again gave us the thumbs up.

The first time we played Gilman, a friend in the crowd recorded our set. That friend happened to be standing next to Tim Yohannan, and I was so happy when I got home to hear Tim clearly on the tape cracking up uncontrollably ("ha Ha! HA!!! HAAAAAA!!!") during my vituperative-filled diatribes. Tim got me. He understood what we were doing, and appreciated it.

Several days after Tim's death, Jughead faxed me a few sheets of press clippings for *Major Label Debut*. Tim had given the record a really great review, even going as far as to say that the record might be my "rebirth." I felt the usual surge of pride over the review, and a moment or two later, I practically started crying. I'm glad Tim got it once again.

When I first started writing for MRR in 1988, doing Chicago scene reports, Tim encouraged me, if only by assuming that if I could string a couple of sentences together I must've known what I was doing. If he was lacking as an editor (he never gave input — in fact, he seldom even read anything, including his own magazine), at least he never told me what to write or what not to write. I was left to sink or swim on my own, and while learning how to write in public can be ugly (or in my case, brutal), I was grateful for the opportunity to have my words read by more than 10,000 people each month.

In the beginning, I was promised a column only every other month. Once the hate mail started pouring in from my first column, Tim called up to tell me I could write one every month if I liked. Tim had great respect for shit-disturbers and rabble-rousers — people after his own heart. As I kept writing for MRR, I got to know him and we became friends. He never stopped challenging me. I learned from him not to buy into my own bullshit, and not to believe other people's hype about me. I learned about the concepts of a band's accountability and responsibility. I learned the reality that most of the time when people throw up their hands and claim that they *have* to do business as usual because there's no other choice, they're really just not willing to make the effort anymore. I've always tried to remember those things.

Naturally, Tim disagreed. If Tim were to have a headstone, that's how it should've read: TIM DISAGREED. In the last few years, he claimed that I'd become cynical. In fact, he claimed that my cynicism was a bigger factor behind his canning me as an MRR columnist than was the fact that my band had gone on tour with Green Day (the latter being the official reason). And I felt that Tim was mostly wrong. He started doing more and more things that pissed me off, or maybe I just started noticing them.

The problem was that Tim held everyone to his own standards. I learned long ago that if you do that, everyone's going to disappoint you. Tim didn't care. He *knew* what was right, even when he was dead fucking wrong, and he stood up for what he believed. The guy had twelve-pound Brunswicks for balls. You had to admire him.

For my part, I was pissed at Tim for running (and, in my opinion, penning) a gossip column in which punk scene luminaries were slammed by persons unknown; the column was run under a pseudonym and the author(s) was a highly-guarded secret. To me, the attitude behind the column was the antithesis of what I'd always respected about MRR. One of the reasons I'd always wanted to write for the mag was because the columnists could say whatever they wanted, even if Tim didn't agree. But they had to be somewhat *accountable* for their words; using a pseudonym was one thing but concealing your identity was quite another. You had to accept the fact that what you wrote might cause you to get punched in the nose. Granted, there are times when keeping one's identity a secret is necessary, but I didn't believe the gossip column served either a true comedic or muckraking purpose. Tim disagreed, or at least didn't give a fuck.

So I was canned from the magazine, I withdrew my support of it because of the gossip column, and to this day MRR refuses to run Panic Button ads due to our affiliation with Lookout Records. But we remained friends.

Tim was second only to the Ramones in terms of his influence on punk rock, and a close second at that. He was the single most important force in shaping what punk means. But he was a great guy, too, which is why when he acted like an asshole I didn't just tell him to go fuck himself and tear his name out of my Rolodex (and it's probably why he didn't tear *my* name out of *his* address book when I acted like an asshole).

The reason Tim was able to accomplish so much was because of his boundless energy, which I believe was fueled by a serious anger at the way the human race chooses to behave. That energy was contagious. I remember sitting in Tim's living room — which was actually the main office for MRR — and bitching about the magazine's apparent lack of desire to *really* question the business practices of some then-popular bands and labels. Tim suggested that I get off my fat ass and do it myself. I said I would if he'd back me up. And so we sat there puffing away on our cigarettes, formulating a plan for what would become the briefly famous "Business Of Punk" issue of MRR. Tim paid my expenses and sent me out the door, and the result had a much bigger effect than I'd ever anticipated. Tim understood that one of his best qualities was the ability to organize and motivate people; he made things happen. MRR. Gilman. Blacklist. Epicenter.

But if you were just hanging around the MRR house, Tim was a ball. As Mykel Board has already noted in his comments after Tim's death, Tim had the most genuine, beautiful laugh. For me, there was a sense of approval in that laugh. When Tim thought I was full of shit, his voice took on a wary tone. But when he thought I was right on, and particularly when I was venting about one thing or another, he let loose with an enormous, joyous belly laugh of the type that simply can't be faked.

I'll never forget watching him jump around the room — a 45-year-old guy — playing air guitar, stoked beyond belief over the first New Bomb Turks record. Or the time I made an offhand comment about how good my band's drummer was, and Tim dragged me down to the basement, dug through the stacks of records (the man had thousands of records filling shelves that covered three walls of an enormous room, every single one of them covered on the spine, top and bottom with thick green tape for reasons that only Tim knew), found the rare Velvet Underground record he was looking for, put it on the turntable and cued up a song and said, "Listen to this! THIS is great drumming!"

One summer when I was staying at the house I flipped on the All-Star game. Tim watched for a while, and then went into the next room. He came back holding a torn and battered program from a ballgame (was it the New York Giants? I can't remember now...) he had been to see with his father when he was a kid. He looked kind of embarrassed about having kept the thing, but I was impressed. That was just one of several little signs I saw over the years that despite his dislike of maudlin displays and romanticism, Tim was hardly an automaton or a Scrooge; he was a regular guy like the rest of us.

Whether we were eating some greasy takeout food (Tim *never* cooked), arguing about music or politics, playing backgammon or watching a video, Tim was always fun to be around. I was always grateful for his friendship. Even when I was canned from MRR, and every other person I ran into was asking me how I felt about it, I couldn't say anything but, "I'm surprised he didn't do it sooner." And it was the truth. Tim canned me because he felt he *had* to. But he told me straight out that he felt bad about it, and I know he did. It was just Tim holding me up to his standards again.

I was planning on visiting him before he died. I wanted to give him a hug — Tim, despite his reputation, was a big hugger — and tell him how important he was to me, and let him know that he really changed my life and helped me become a better person. I know Tim didn't believe in God and I don't either, so I don't think he's somewhere above watching me. But I'd like to think that he knew how I felt about him.

I talked to Tim two weeks before he died. When I asked how he was doing, and he answered "Not too good," I finally realized he didn't have much longer. I let him know that I was going to be in the Bay Area in a few weeks. I was trying to tell him to hold on, without coming out and saying it. It didn't matter. I didn't get to hug Tim before he died, and I didn't get to tell him all the things I wanted to tell him (although thankfully, I did get to tell him a lot in the time after he was diagnosed with lymphoma).

I loved the guy, and I cried when I heard he died, and I've cried several times since then. Tim will be missed by people who never even met him; those who understand his influence on punk rock, as well as their own lives. Those of us who knew him will miss him for those reasons, but we'll also miss being able to go over to the MRR house and hang out with him, a simple act that often resulted in a surge of one's own energy and excitement about punk rock music and politics.

As much of a pain in the ass as he could be, and as rotten as he was capable of acting sometimes, Tim was ultimately one of the good guys, and he was an inspiration. And even though he didn't go in for sentimentality, I don't think he'd find anything corny about people acknowledging the fact that the world is a shittier place without him. Fuck, I miss the cranky old bastard already.

THE RUNAWAY

I was fourteen years old the first time I ran away from home. I was hanging out in The Pit — the school's outdoor smoking area — at what was known as Homo High with my friend Phil. Phil was the same age as me but he looked older; he was a big Greek with the same feelings of hatred and frustration that I had about being forced to attend an all-boy's Catholic high school.

It was one of those boring, cold days when the sun is shining but it's still only about 35 degrees outside. We had nothing to smoke but cigarettes and we both somehow decided that going back to class after lunch was a dumb idea.

"Let's run away," I said brightly.

"Yeah!" said Phil, probably more out of a need to show he wasn't afraid than anything else.

My next-door neighbor Tom had recently moved down to Nashville. He was in his twenties, and a cool enough guy. I'd talked about running away a zillion times before and he'd always told me not to come to his house if I ever did, but I figured he'd change his mind once he saw us at his doorstep.

I was all for leaving right then, but Phil had to stop by his house.

"My leg's all fucked up," he said. "I gotta get my antibiotics from home."

Phil lived about a mile or so from our school, right behind the public high school, John Hersey. We walked to his house and got his antibiotics. Then he said he wanted to stop by Hersey.

I was starting to get impatient. It was already 2:00.

"I gotta see my sister and tell her I'm going," he said. "She'll be all pissed off if I leave and don't tell her."

Jesus, this was getting ridiculous. I tried to act all stern.

"Don't let her talk you out of it."

"I won't."

"We're going, y'know. Your sister's gonna try to talk you out of it, but we're going."

"I know, I know."

We hung out near the main entrance of the school until the last class was out. Phil walked around trying to find his sister. He finally saw one of her friends and got her to go get the elusive sister.

When sis showed up, she didn't really try to talk him out of it too much. I could tell she sort of thought it was cool. He said his goodbyes and we left. Once we were outside the school, he pulled three twenties from his pocket.

"Where'd you get that?"

"My sister gave it to me. I guess it wasn't such a dumb idea to stop here, was it?"

Having $1.25 to my name, I was in no position to argue.

We walked and walked and walked. We had our thumbs out there in the cold for three hours but nobody picked us up. We were headed in what we thought was the general direction of a highway, but we couldn't be sure. At around 5:30 we stopped at a gas station and got a map. We were right by I-294, which, according to the map, led down to highway 80. From there it was just a quick jaunt to I-65 south, which went right into Nashville. We walked up the on-ramp, sat on a guardrail and stuck out our thumbs. Within a couple of minutes, we were picked up and got a ride down to some unfamiliar exit. We got off and tried thumbing again. No luck. We started walking down Ogden Avenue and soon saw a sign informing us we were in Downers Grove. I consulted my map but I couldn't find the town. We kept walking. We walked for hours, stopping only to eat a couple of 25-cent hamburgers at McDonald's — they had a special going for Valentine's Day weekend.

As it got colder and darker, I suggested that we look for a motel. We stopped at five of them. The first four refused to give us a room because we had no I.D. to prove we were eighteen. The last motel was next to an I-

HOP. The old guy behind the counter didn't wanna give us a room, but we laid the pity stuff on him pretty hard and he relented. In a couple of minutes we were in the room watching TV.

The next morning, we were out of the room and eating breakfast in the I-HOP by 8:00. After we finished, Phil got a box of Marlboros for each of us. We sat smoking and drinking water, sort of hanging around avoiding the inevitable.

"Do you wanna go home?" he asked.

"No," I said. And I didn't. But I wasn't too excited about the idea of standing out on the highway all day. We hadn't been too lucky with rides last night, so I didn't think we had much chance to make it to Nashville by tonight. I thought about it for a while and then gave him as much of a pep talk as I could muster. We headed back out on Ogden toward the highway.

This time, we'd been on the ramp for only a few minutes when we got a ride. The guy was a real prick though, telling us to watch the upholstery and whatnot, being a real pain in the ass. He finally let us out on an off ramp just off of I-65. As I was getting out of the car, the door handle came off in my hand. I don't even know how, I mean, I didn't do anything but open the fucking door. The guy got all pissed off but we just laughed at him; he was backing up traffic and had no way to go but forward.

After only a few minutes, a big Cadillac pulled up and we climbed in. The back seat was huge and the machine was being skippered by a forty-ish guy wearing an expensive looking suit and reeking of Old Spice and arrogance. I gave him the standard speech about how we were running away 'cause our parents were fucked, making sure to tell the guy that Phil's parents beat him regularly. It wasn't true, but it was good for sympathy.

He started talking about drugs, asking if we had any Rush or Locker Room. He was really into poppers. He kept talking and talking about them; all the time cranking out his Beethoven or whatever the hell classical shit he was listening to. Phil asked him to change the station once (and I elbowed him in the ribs good for THAT one) but he just said, "This is wonderful music, you can really appreciate it when you're speeding." I made up a story about me being a big-time speed dealer in Chicago and having to get out of it 'cause of the law. The idiot bought it. He woulda bought anything. He was the kinda guy who would buy an ounce of pure oregano from you, then call you up the next week and thank you for the great dope.

He drove us pretty far, all the way down to Louisville, but I think he finally dumped us 'cause he was getting annoyed; we were fucking around in the back seat and making fun of him behind his back. I knew it wasn't a bright move, but the guy was so flaky and flamboyant and silly, I couldn't help it. And Phil had no concept of tact at any time.

We walked down the highway for about an hour until some burn-out guys in a black Camaro picked us up. They asked us if we had any weed and we told them we didn't. Two miles later we were back pounding the pavement.

"Fucking assholes anyway," I said.

"Yeah, we shoulda told 'em we had pot."

Phil was starting to irritate me. "If we told 'em we had pot, they'd want some. Then what?"

"Then nothing. We'd kick the shit out of them."

I didn't bother mentioning that these guys woulda slaughtered us. Phil always got a little pissy when his own stupidity was pointed out to him.

We were outside a town called Shepherdsville, in Kentucky. We wandered down the street off the highway until we found a McDonald's. We were almost broke. We had gone through a drive-thru with the Cadillac guy and spent way too much money. We bought a pack of cigarettes and had enough dough left for two 25-cent hamburgers.

I went up and ordered and the girl behind the counter asked where we were from.

"Chicago," I said, tired of answering the same old questions. "We ran away from home." She was really nice to us, and when she handed our bag to us, it was crammed full of burgers and fries. We practically kissed her, then slinked off to a corner to wolf down the food. We hung around the McDonald's smoking and bullshitting until it was starting to feel like we didn't have the guts to get back out and hitch. We headed out into the cold again. For some reason, I thought that it would get warmer after we crossed the state line into Kentucky. After all, this was the South.

We got back on the highway at around 7:30 P.M. and started walking. We walked for miles, every so often having to cross a bridge, and of course every time we did, a few trucks would barrel past leaving us literally shaking, feeling like we were about to be knocked to our death.

It was mean-cold now, and totally dark but for the occasional set of headlights. We had been walking for what seemed like hours; neither of us had a watch, but I'd occasionally count up to a minute and start over in a lame attempt to keep track of time. Things looked bad. We had no money for a room and cars were whipping by as if they didn't see us. Phil kept lagging behind, complaining about the pain in his leg. I kept walking faster, trying to keep warm.

We were getting desperate. The trucks seemed to be coming closer to the shoulder and no one gave any signs of pulling over. My thumb was almost frozen from hanging there in the cold. I prayed, literally. I didn't even really believe in God, but I was so fucking low I prayed for a car to pick us up. And about twenty seconds after I finished my little prayer, a car pulled over.

It was a green Charger, a real studmobile. We ran up to the car, pulled open the door and dove into the back seat: "THANKYOUTHANKYOUTHANKYOU." The guy driving the car was black. His name was Leroy and he was from Kankakee, driving down to Atlanta to see his brother or something.

"Got any weed?" he asked.

"No, sorry," I said, every muscle in my body clenched up in a one-man attempt to access his brain with my fervent "DON'T KICK US OUT DON'T KICK US OUT DON'T KICK US OUT" mental chant. He didn't kick us out.

Instead, he talked amiably with us. I looked at the clock on the dash. It was 10:30. We'd spent three hours out in the freezing cold, waiting for a ride. After about an hour, Leroy pulled over to get gas. When he came back from the cashier's, he had big foot long hot dogs and a six-pack of Schlitz Malt Liquor 16-ouncers. We were in hog heaven. We ate and drank heartily, our spirits dampened only by the fact that we had no cigarettes left. Leroy was more than happy to bum us a few. When we got to Nashville, he dumped us at a Denny's and gave us a pack of his Salems.

I swaggered into the Denny's, still slightly drunk from my two beers, and whipped open the phone book in the lobby. Tom's name was nowhere in the book. I called Information. No luck. He had just moved down so maybe he didn't have a phone yet.

Our moment of glory, shattered. We were fucked and we knew it. It was just about then that Phil noticed the sticker on the side of the phone booth.

"Let's call," he said.

"The RUNAWAY HOTLINE???" I almost screamed. "They'll turn us in! We'll spend the night in jail!"

"Well, we're not sleeping here," he said, which was obvious. The Denny's employees were already shooting us nasty looks.

I called. A man answered and I told him we were runaways and needed a place to stay.

"Where are you?" he asked.

I looked out the window at the street sign. "Murfreesboro Road," I answered.

"Okay," he said, "There's a Mission on Murfreesboro, just go left and walk down until you see it."

"How far?" I asked.

"I don't know," he said, "I've never been to Nashville."

We started the long walk. The place was nowhere in sight. We were starting to get into a lousy area too. We walked by a club that was just closing down. A well-dressed older guy was getting into his car. I asked if he knew where the Mission was and he offered to give us a ride. We were there in a few minutes.

We walked in and were shown to our sleeping quarters. We both had top bunks in a six-man room. The walls were painted puke green. Everyone was already asleep. The guy below me was snoring like a sow. The guy under Phil had no legs. Cockroaches scampered merrily on the walls.

"Should we get outta here?" I asked.

"I'm too tired," said Phil. "I gotta sleep."

We fell asleep after about an hour of whispering back and forth about the creepiness of the place. We were woken up after what seemed like a minute and a half. It was 6:00 A.M. and some old guy with a deformed face was telling us to eat some slop in a green bowl. It appeared to be fresh mucus. We declined and got out of there despite his protests. The security guard guy made a half-assed attempt to keep us from leaving but we just ran off and he was in no shape or mood to chase us.

It was Sunday morning, so maybe everyone was at church. The only things on Murfreesboro Road were smashed booze bottles and puddles of blood and vomit. We headed back the way we came from. Phil saw a Greyhound station and suggested we go in for a nap.

We walked into the Greyhound terminal and lay down on two benches. Just as I was drifting off to sleep, I heard a voice.

"You guys run away from home?"

It was a friendly, clean-cut looking fellow, mid-thirties maybe, neatly trimmed mustache, short black hair.

Phil, of course, was involved in a conversation with him already. I pulled him aside.

"He says we can go to his house and crash," Phil said.

I figured the guy was probably okay. He was just a decent guy who had been waiting at the Greyhound station for his friend whose bus hadn't showed up.

"Okay, let's go," I said.

As soon as we got into the guy's car, I smelled a rat. His junky old shitmobile was covered with fast food wrappers and dirty snotrags. He started telling us about his knife that he had got in the war or some such shit.

"Cool," I said absentmindedly.

"You don't believe me?" he said, and he pulled out a big switchblade.

Phil thought it was cool. I thought we'd best not piss this creep off.

We got to his house and on the way to the door, he explained that he really lived in the basement but his doctor friend owned the house and didn't mind him hanging out upstairs. Always thinking ahead, I told him that we had to make a phone call to Chicago soon 'cause we had friends there who could hook us up with a place to stay in Nashville.

When we walked in, the first thing we saw was a huge Doberman sitting inside a cage in the middle of the floor.

"I'd better not let him out," The Creep said as the animal growled at us angrily. "You guys like MTV?"

Sure, we liked MTV — it was still fairly new back then and pretty cool to a couple of fourteen-year-old delinquents.

Phil and I sat down on a love seat in front of the TV and watched lame-ass Duran Duran.

"You want something to drink?" asked The Creep.

"A glass of water would be good," I said.

"Oh c'mon, how about something a little stronger? Rum and Coke?"

It was 6:30 in the morning for chrissakes. Phil jumped at the chance for alcohol. The Creep came over with two huge glasses of rum and Coke, mostly rum. I hated hard liquor and this stuff tasted like shit. Phil was gulping his down. The Creep had been offering us a shower on the way over. Now he was telling us he'd be happy to run a bath for us.

"I don't take baths," I said, "I could really use a shower though."

"The shower's broken."

"Oh well, I'll pass...."

Phil was oblivious. The Creep left for a minute and came back carrying a pair of satin shorts in each hand.

"Y'all would be more comfortable in these," he said.

Sirens, bells, flashing lights.

"I don't think so," I said.

"Yeah, we're fine," said Phil, a funny little quizzical look on his face. I was sitting on the left side of the couch, Phil on the right. The Creep had been sitting on the edge of the couch by Phil. Now he squeezed in next to him. Pat Benatar was on MTV asking us to hit her with our best shot.

"Man, she's hot," said Phil.

"Oh yeah, " said The Creep. "There's nothing like a big, wet tongue around your dick."

Sirens went off in my head once again. I vowed to play it cool. No sudden moves.

"Yep," he continued, "Nothing like a nice piece of ass."

"Or a nice, wet pussy," I offered.

He wasn't impressed. "Sure you don't want to put these on?" he said, waving the shorts. "I really think you could use a nice warm bath and a change of clothes."

Phil was finally beginning to catch on, the dolt. He put down his glass and shot me a look. The Creep went to the kitchen for a minute and Phil leaned over to me.

"He's weird," he said.

"No shit," I answered. "He's a fuckin' homo. He wants our asses."

Phil gave me a questioning look and wiggled his wrist in faglike fashion.

"Lemme do the talking," I said. "Whatever I say, you agree. We gotta get outta here." My only hope was that if the guy got rough, Phil would clock him good. He was only fourteen, but he was a pretty tough guy.

The Creep came back and continued urging us to take baths and get into his queer little shorts. I'd occasionally comment about the fact that it was almost time for us to make our call. I kept watching the digital clock on top of the TV, waiting for it to hit 6:55. I had decided that's when we were leaving.

The Creep was getting creepier, making vaguely threatening references to his knife and his dog. Finally the time came.

"We gotta make that call," I said. "Is there a pay phone around here?"

"Well there's one right down at the corner," he answered. "But you can call from here."

FUCK!!! I thought fast. "Well, it's a long distance call."

"That's alright," he said. "Just keep it short."

I had him now. "Well, the thing is, I gotta get directions from this girl and it's gonna take a long time." That sounded good. Now to add a little fuel to the fire. "Plus my girlfriend is over there and she's gonna wanna talk to me."

He looked reluctant, but I could tell he didn't want us making a long call to Chicago. He gave us long, drawn out directions to the phone booth on the corner. We were almost at the door when he did a little hop and wound up in front of us.

"Y'all comin' back, right?" he asked. The dog was barking now, sounding like it wouldn't mind chewing on our nuts.

"Oh yeah," said Phil. "We're just gonna make this phone call and then we'll come right back."

The Creep looked suspicious, but he unlocked the door and let us go. We walked down the steps and onto the street. As soon as we were past the house, we ran.

About a block later, we were still running, but cracking up.

"This is gonna make a great story," said Phil. "But when we tell it, let's say you kicked the guy in the balls and I punched him in the face."

I agreed and we kept running until we were back on Murfreesboro. We were even farther away from civilization than before. At least there were cop cars whizzing by every ten seconds. We were on the middle of a bridge when I looked back and saw The Creep behind us in his car. He saw me spot him and yelled, "Hey, where ya goin'? What's the matter?"

We both gave him the finger and yelled "Fuck you, homo," and other such clever insults at him. He looked pretty pissed off so we started running. By the time we were off the bridge and halfway through a vacant lot, we realized he had turned around.

We kept walking down Murfreesboro, but now Phil was really whining about his leg. At one point, I turned around to see him two blocks behind me. We kept stopping so he could rest but it was getting ridiculous.

After what seemed like twenty miles, we reached the Denny's where we had been dumped the night before.

"I'm going home," said Phil. "I'm gonna call my dad and have him pick me up. You can go too."

"You PUSSY!" I shouted. "What the fuck is wrong with you? We made it, we're here!"

"We're never gonna find Tom," he said. "He's not even in the phonebook." He was probably right, but I spent about twenty minutes trying to talk him out of it anyway. It was no good. He gave me half a pack of Salems and two dollars he had swiped from The Creep's house. I turned my back and kept walking.

After a while I stopped at a 7-11 type joint called the Hot Spot and bought a soda. I hung around for a while until the guy behind the counter got suspicious.

I spilled my guts to him and told him if I could just use his phone to call Chicago, I'd be outta there.

He let me into the back room and I called Tom's mother's house, hoping to reach his sister. Of course, I got his mother instead. She told me she didn't have the number but that she'd call me back. I gave her the number at the Hot Spot and went back out to browse around magazines and stuff. When she called back, she said she had spoken to my parents and that if I wanted to come home, I had to call Judy somebody, some friend of my parents from their Toughlove group. Fuck that.

"Sorry," I said. "I'm not coming home." I thought maybe I could get a job at the Hot Spot and sleep in the storeroom for a while. The guy behind the counter was the manager and he seemed to like me.

We got to talking and he told me after his shift I could come to his house for dinner. He lived with his wife, her sister and her sister's husband. I was a bit skeptical after having narrowly escaped the clutches of John Wayne Gacy's country cousin, but having no other real choice, I reluctantly agreed. I figured if there was no sister and husband when we got there I'd run like hell. He was a skinny, wimpy guy who looked like he didn't do much running.

He bought me a hot dog, and when his shift ended we got into his car and headed for his house. I was pretty happy, I mean, he'd bought me a pack of cigarettes (but he got Salems, 'cause that's what I had been smoking) and he seemed okay.

He lived in a nice little ranch house in the suburbs. Walking in was like entering the Walton's at Christmastime. The manager was a born-again Christian and so was everyone who lived there. Well, at least they made a big spaghetti dinner. I sat down and dug in.

"Ummm... we say grace before we eat." It was the guy's wife. I felt my face turning red.

The brother-in-law spoke up. "Do YOU want to say grace?"

"Uh, I don't really know any prayers," I said. All I knew was GODISGREATGODISGOOD and something told me that wouldn't cut it with these Jesus jumpers. Somebody said a big long prayer and then we ate. Well, sort of. I mean, it was the worst spaghetti I'd ever had, like out of a can. I forced as much into myself as possible before giving up.

"Not hungry?" asked the manager.

"No, I don't eat much," I said, which was only a half lie anyway.

After dinner I went out to the backyard for a smoke. When I came back inside, they let me shower and gave me a pair of pajamas that were way too big. I hated pajamas but I put them on to please them. They also convinced me to call those friends of my parents. I did and it was worked out that I'd fly back the next day, Valentine's Day, and get picked up by these mysterious friends. Then they gave me some comic books and pulled out the couchbed for me. As soon as they went to bed, I ditched the crummy jammies and fell asleep.

The next day I was woken up early to make the 10:00 A.M. flight to Chicago. The manager and his family waited for me at the airport until I was about to board the plane. Then they gave me a hug and their names and phone number on a card and told me to call them collect after I'd gotten back and settled in. It was really weird; I mean these people really acted like they LIKED me.

It was only a forty-five minute flight. A pudgy lady and her sheepish looking husband met me at O'Hare. I got in their car and after a while I realized we weren't heading towards my house.

"Where are we going?" I asked.

"You'll see when we get there," was the only answer I got to that oft-repeated question.

They were Toughlove parents, and they explained that their daughter was the problem child in their family. Right, I'd have to look her up. We pulled up in front of a Marine Recruiting Center in Palatine. They took me inside and left. A big marine took me into a small back room with an empty desk and two chairs. Immediately the guy started screaming at me. The usual crap, about how I was an ungrateful little asshole, I was killing my parents, etc. He was right up in my face, little flecks of his spit hitting me in the nose. I just sat there and took it. Then he ordered me to empty my pockets.

I did as he said. He told me to take the pin off my jacket. I laid it down on the table. He pulled out a manila envelope, wrote "PERSONAL EFFECTS" on it in big block letters and started doing an inventory on a sheet of paper.

"One comb, black," he said in his professional military voice. I smirked at him and he squinted his beady little eyes at me.

"I could kick the living shit out of you right now and there's not a goddamn thing you can do about it," he said quietly.

I didn't believe him. "I dare you," I said.

More in-my-face roaring from the prick.

"I'm not going into the army," I said.

This enraged him more than anything else. "YOU'RE TALKING TO A GODDAMN MARINE!!!" he screamed. "YOU ADDRESS ME AS SIR!"

"Yessir," I mumbled.

He sat back down and continued his inventory.

"37 cents, change. One Zippo lighter." He opened it up and pulled out the fluid filter, finding nothing of course. I was surprised that he was savvy enough to know that it was a good place to stash things like speed or small amounts of pot. He put the Zippo back together and dropped it in the envelope.

"One wallet, brown. One mairjawanna leaf pin, gold." This he dropped into the wastebasket.

"Hey," I said. "Whattya think you're doing?"

"You don't want your father to see that, do you?"

"Fuck that," I said. "Give it back." He put it into the envelope reluctantly, writing "1 Dope Leaf" on the envelope.

After he finished, he left the room and I sat there alone for five hours until my old man showed up. He put me in the car, handing me my personal effects envelope minus my pin, lighter and cigarettes. Then he drove me to my uncle's apartment in Highland Park, where I spent the next three days sitting on the couch doing nothing, occasionally getting my aunt to turn her back so I could cop a few drags from her cigarette.

Finally I was picked up by the old man and brought home. I got a three hour-long lecture about how things were gonna change and all that bullshit. After it was over, I said, "No way," walked outside and started off down the street. Hell, it was my first night back in town. I had to have a little fun.

THE PAPER BOY

I started working for the agency in early January. That's about the worst time of the year for that type of work in Chicago, and it didn't help that I was studying to become a professional alcoholic. I had just quit my job on the graveyard shift at the gas station and the money I had saved had run out.

The ad in the paper sounded great. Good money, short hours and little supervision. I'd never had a paper route as a kid and I'd always regretted it. This was the job for me.

I filled out an application at the agency in Wheeling. Sandy, the owner, explained that her husband had recently died and that she had inherited the agency. She really didn't know what she was doing yet. So much the better for me. I would be given a route with 270 dailies and 380 Sundays. I could start that night.

I came in at 2:00 AM and waited for Sandy's son in the warehouse — he'd be showing me the ropes. He walked up and introduced himself, explaining that we had some time to kill until the trucks came in. Jim talked a lot about various drugs. He was really into smoking pot. I'd long since given up such drugs so I wasn't really interested — nice enough guy, but nothing to say. Finally, the trucks pulled in and everybody rushed over to the garage door. The guys on the truck threw down bundles of papers that came in numbers ranging from twenty to fifty, depending on the size of that day's issue. I grabbed five bundles each of main sections plus the Tempo sections that were inserted.

I brought the bundles of papers back to the worktable against the far wall of the warehouse, sliced off the plastic ties and watched as Jim showed me how to stuff them. You put a stack of papers to your left and a stack of inserts to your right or behind them, whichever way went quicker. A bunch of plastic bags hung on a nail near the edge of the table. Stuff a paper with an insert, cram it in a bag, tear off the bag and toss it into a big, canvas cart. It took about 45 minutes. After I was done, I went and opened the garage door and backed my '76 Malibu into the bay. Except for Sundays, Jim told me, I'd be able to fit most of the papers in my back seat. After I loaded my car, he handed me my clipboard and we took off.

My route had three sections. The first was a huge maze of a subdivision filled with quad-type houses. Each driveway served four different buildings in cul-de-sac fashion. The second section was the worst. It was a series of townhouses, laid out in such a way that short, dead end streets led to parking spaces at the rear of the buildings. The third section was a subdivision filled with regular houses, and though it was the biggest part of the run, it was the easiest.

Jim went with me my first two nights and showed me how to use a highlight pen to mark porch services and people out of town. I got the hang of it pretty quick.

I worked in the warehouse stuffing papers next to a guy named Frank, who was an older guy from McHenry with a family, and Mikey, who was a foul-mouthed mailman from Buffalo Grove. Most of the people who worked at the agency had real jobs during the day. It sounded like fun. Get up at 2:00 AM to make it to the agency at 2:30 AM, work until 5:30 or 6 (most of the guys had larger routes than mine), go off to work an eight hour day, then come home to a quick dinner, maybe a little TV and off to bed. Fuck that; this was going to be my sole source of income.

Frank was a pretty nice guy. He mostly kept to himself but he made a little small talk now and then. He processed credit card applications at his day job and he gave me some tips on how even a bum like me with bad credit could get a card with a big credit line. Mikey was a real bigmouth, but a lovable bigmouth. He started calling me Bobby on the first day. I wore an old army jacket and had recently shaved off my mohawk and he claimed I resembled Robert DeNiro in *Taxi Driver* (I'd gotten the same thing at the gas station, drunken jerks stumbling in and asking me where my cab was). "That's right," I'd tell him. "And one of these days, I'm gonna clean up all this filth and shit and scum..."

Mikey really had it in for the people on his mail route. He'd come in almost every night griping about some woman on his route.

"That goddamn Jew bitch," he'd grumble. "Sittin' in her house with her fuckin' money, just waiting for me to come by so she can bitch about her fuckin' mail again." He was massive and often drunk. Mikey was a pretty impressive sight when he'd come in at 2:30 in the morning, hair flying wildly, booming about that fuckin' Jew bitch... He was a real character, always had some wisecrack to make about anyone who would pass him by, but he was always pretty cool with everyone at the agency.

The problem was, Mikey just couldn't stand working for the public. Maybe it was the post office that turned him off of people, but there were a few "wise guys" on his route and Mikey refused to cater to them. The owner, Sandy, was a pretty nice lady — maybe too nice — and I really felt sorry for her whenever she had to deal with Mikey. She'd leave the complaint sheets on his clipboard above his route sheets and man, if there was a little pink slip on his route sheet, he'd fly into a rage. "That motherfucker!" he'd scream. "I see that piece of shit looking at me from behind his window every goddamn morning, but he don't have the balls to say shit to me!!" Inevitably, Sandy would come around and he'd lay into her good. He always started talking to her in midsentence: "He's just trying to fuck with me! I mean, pardon my language, but he's an asshole!"

Sandy always tried to placate him, but it was a losing battle. "I know Mikey, but it's not me. The *Tribune* says we have to give you the complaints."

He never really seemed to hear her. Her explanations simply served as intermissions for him to collect his hostile thoughts. "That prick calls if his fuckin' paper is two goddamn inches into the sidewalk. I can't slow down my whole route for this bastard, he ruins my pace." And he'd bitch and bitch and sometimes keep on throwing the guy's paper a little short just to show him he wouldn't be pushed around.

"I swear to God, Bobby," he used to tell me. "Any day now I'm gonna go over there in the middle of the day and pound the shit out of him!"

I had my own problems in the warehouse. For one, the lifers — the guys who had been doing this shit since they were born and would continue for another fifty years — always muscled their way to the front of the trucks when the papers arrived. There was an unspoken but very serious and complicated system in place whereby certain guys got their papers first and boy, if a young, wise bastard like me ever took the first bundle... well I'd probably end up stabbed with a carton opener. As a result, I often got the really torn, fucked up papers, and a lot of times I'd come up short, cause the Trib didn't give a rat's ass if they sent twenty papers too few. Eventually, I worked out a deal where I'd worm my way in between the lifers and the kids. Actually, they weren't all kids who weren't old enough to have routes, but most were (one of the guys was actually on a sort of probation from his route cause he had gotten so many speeding tickets and DUI's). They just stuffed papers, stacked them for guys with box routes and put together the supplements for the Thursday and Sunday papers. They were pretty goddamn cutthroat about getting their papers but the DUI guy somehow knew about my band and would always grab a few bundles for me. To tell you the truth, he kind of got on my nerves, always talking to me about music and the band and stuff, but he was a valuable ally in the bundle battles.

Working in the warehouse sucked but I trained myself to whip through my bagging in record time and I was usually about the fourth or fifth person out the door. One thing you never did was attempt to go out the opposite side garage door while Mikey was working. Even if he wasn't close to being done, Mikey would flip out if somebody used that door when he was bagging, cause that was, like, HIS goddamn door. I ended up using it a lot cause Mikey bagged way quicker than me and was almost always done loading his 340-paper route before I was even done bagging my measly 270.

I saw a couple of guys make the mistake of fucking up Mikey's pace by loading just as he was finishing bagging. Mikey didn't like to wait. He'd pull up his van right in front of whoever's car was being loaded so they'd have to really squirm their way out and he'd glare at them the whole time. If I thought I'd even come close to fucking up Mikey's pace, I'd just stand there and wait until the other bay was open.

All the guys were really territorial too. Like the time I had a shitload of Thursdays and they crossed over about two inches into Mikey's territory (He had about 18 more feet of space to work in than I did, as did Frank) and he just came over, hair all flying and said, "Bobby, Bobby, Bobby, you're one of the good guys, now don't make me move those papers for you." He didn't have to.

The route wasn't so bad, except for the first two sections where I had to constantly back up and creep forward. It was a sonofabitch for me to wing papers out the passenger window. I mean, try it one time, using your right arm to hold your steering wheel, and your left to wing a paper about twenty feet, moving at about two miles per hour. It's pretty hard to make an accurate throw. All of the quad houses had porch service so I always had to make near-stops; I'd pull up into the space closest to the porches and be winging the papers and shifting into reverse at the same time, if possible. A lot of the time, though, I'd have three or four papers to throw on a porch so I'd have to come to a complete stop. And often, somebody would be parked in the space closest to the porch, so I'd have to pull in next to the car and whip the papers over it. I NEVER got out of my car. I didn't care if I threw my goddamn arm out; it was a matter of pride. I wouldn't place some asshole's paper on his porch (except for one guy, and I'll get to him later).

The townhouses sucked because there was such little room down those tiny streets. If there were cars in the driveways I had to be careful that the papers didn't go sliding underneath. They'd always complain. I had pretty good aim, so I'd technically be able to make them from the street, but I always had to turn around in a driveway because of the lack of space. Usually, I'd pull up in the furthest space, fling my papers for that side, then back into a space at the building on the other side of the street and do the same. It was a pretty fast way to do it, but I still had to waste a lot of time backing up, slowing down and making three-point turns.

In the subdivision, I could get up some good speed, and since I had my route memorized for Monday through Saturday, I knew just the right point to fling the paper over the top of my car with my left hand so it landed smack in the driveway. It always had to be at least past the sidewalk. The only thing that fucked that up was the jerks that had porch service. I'd be cruising along at a nice clip and then have to screw it all up by pulling into some bum's driveway and whipping his lousy paper on the porch. What kind of person is it, I often wondered, who is so lazy that he can't even walk twelve feet to get his paper? What a world we live in.

Acts of nature didn't mean shit to the Trib. I was out in more than one blizzard, window wide open, streets unplowed, barely able to see two feet in front of me, let alone where the sidewalk started, but you were expected to do it right every time, otherwise you got written up. I got seven complaints one night after my perfectly delivered Tuesday papers (which were the skinniest ones each week) were whipped around various crybabies' yards by hurricane-type wind conditions. Too bad. If you got written up enough, the Trib forced the agency to fire you.

I worked out a pretty good system, and except for Thursdays and Sundays, when the papers were really thick, I breezed through it in a hour and a half or so and was back home sleeping by five a.m.

Sundays however, were a whole different story, and a pretty ugly one at that. The papers were too large to be folded so they had to be slid into a huge plastic bag. Between the awkward bagging system and the additional 110 papers, bagging took about twice as long, even with my drummer, Brian Vermin, helping me. I paid Brian twenty bucks a week to give me a hand on Sundays because I never would have gotten the route done on time otherwise. The Sundays usually came in later than the rest of the week and between that and the bagging, we wouldn't even get out until 4:30 or 5:00, and we had to be done by 8:00. We always had to make two trips, usually doing the first two sections and then coming back for the subdivision papers.

As I said, I didn't like getting out of my car, but the Sunday papers were way too big to just throw on the porch. Having Vermin along solved that problem; he'd run the papers onto the porches. I have a sort of a sadistic streak in me and it intensifies with loads of coffee and lack of sleep. I used to enjoy sending Vermin out to dump the papers on the quad porches and then speeding away just as he was about to get back to the car. The fact that it was still pretty cold out when he started working with me made it worse. He got fed up with that crap pretty quick and at one point, he whipped a Zinger at me and it splattered all over the dash and clipboard. I figured maybe I should lay off before he got violent.

Because it was a seven-day-a-week job with no days off, the route became my life. I had recently turned twenty-one and had started drinking a lot. Usually, I would finish my route, head home for a six-pack and sleep until mid-afternoon. But a lot of times I'd get totally wacked out in the late evening and attempt to take a nap before work. That just fucked up things even more so most of the time I was walking around in a daze.

I didn't sleep too much that spring; I'd drink so much goddamn coffee on my route that I had to drink beer when I got back home in order to be able to sleep. I often drank at night as well, which would make me more tired; more than once I came into work hung over. It wasn't a big deal — a lot of guys came in completely shitfaced — but it made the work harder. In addition to all of this, working in the warehouse made me sick. The ink got inside you; every morning I would blow my nose for about twenty minutes straight until all the jet-black ink was gone from my snot. I'm sure some of it drained into my stomach; I always had a sickly, vomity feeling in my gut for a couple of hours after my route. Anytime I brought along a friend on the route they'd always end up feeling sick.

But the money was great. And the actual working hours weren't too long. Still, the whole routine became a backbreaker.

Eventually, it warmed up and because of my aversion to deodorant, I got a little more working space at my table (Mikey didn't budge an inch — he wouldn't have cared if I'd smelled of fresh dog shit — but Frank moved a few paces over). But I began getting more complaints on my route and caring less and less.

Over at the quad division, some prick started standing on his porch a few mornings every week while I dumped off the papers. He'd never let me hand the paper to him — I tried once but he just looked at me. No, I had to set it on the porch in front of him so he could bend over and pick it up. Luckily, my hours were such that I didn't have to deal with those kind of jerks often, but just seeing the complaint sheets led me to believe that many of these characters were real assholes, and I didn't care for delivering their goddamn papers to their doorsteps.

I was about to go on tour with the band and there was no way I could keep my job. Vermin dropped out of school and began coming with me a few nights every week, but I couldn't afford to pay him any more than the twenty I'd been paying. We sat around and got drunk a lot and grumbled about the boneheads at the agency.

What really set me off and made me glad to quit was the Sunday morning I was spied on. Mikey had been complaining all week that Trib spies were watching him. I just figured the poor dumb bastard was finally losing what shreds of a mind he possessed. Right. I was about ten papers short of finishing my route (and for some reason that day it was going slow; I was close to the 8:00 deadline) when I noticed the same car that had been parked several blocks away now sitting at the entrance to the cul-de-sac I was currently working in. And there were two big FBI looking pricks sitting in the car watching us.

"Vermin," I said. "Those mooks are spying on us."

"Oh shit," said Vermin. He was never very helpful in crises.

Sure enough, as soon as they saw us pointing they acknowledged our presence. I drove past them and they motioned us to stop. I pulled alongside them and Thing #1 says, "It's almost 8:00."

"Yeah," I said, like I was real bored, "I have three papers left."

I finished the route and went back to the agency. Sure enough, Sandy starts giving me a little lecture as soon as I walk into the door, telling me how me and Vermin shouldn't goof off so much on the route (big deal — we used to have a little fun throwing papers around and Vermin occasionally liked to surf on the hood of my moving vehicle). I worked up a half-hearted attempt at righteous indignation and informed Sandy that those bastards weren't gonna tell me how to do my job.

Thus, between Mikey's complaints and my bitching, poor Sandy was scared to come within fifty yards of our workstation. Even perfect family man Frank got written up and you could almost taste the venom oozing out from our corner of the warehouse. All this served my purpose perfectly and I was able to make quite a dramatic exit about a week later. I just dumped the fucking job. I handed over my clipboard, picked up my check and said adios. And that was the end of my career as a paperboy.

THE JANITOR

On weekends we had to be at the movie theater an hour before opening to get ready for the masses. Often I'd see the cleaning crew finishing up their janitorial work. One morning I overheard the head of the "crew" (he and his wife) complaining about the workload. His wife was pregnant and had recently had to take a job behind the candy counter at the theater. She'd been working with us for a couple of weeks and was fairly pleasant aside from her annoying habit of calling her goddamn husband every five minutes. She was also pretty good at escaping shitty jobs, but I guess we all were.

On this particular morning, Dwight was bitching about the fact that his wife had just worked with him all night and now she had to go work behind the candy counter for six hours. He needed to hire somebody.

Later that day I grilled Mary about the job. It was pretty simple, she told me. Dwight had contracts with our two-screen theater in Mt. Prospect as well as a four-screen theater up in Deerfield. Sunday through Thursday was a breeze — both theaters took a total of four or five hours. The real work came on the weekends. The theaters were more packed, therefore messier, plus we had the distinction of having a midnight showing of the Rocky Horror flick Fridays and Saturdays at our theater. Still, the job sounded simple — cleaning the theaters, bathrooms and lobby. Like all of the jobs I've had, there wasn't a lot of heavy brainwork involved. I told

Mary I'd work for Dwight. She immediately called him and he agreed to pay me five bucks an hour under the table. I had to start that night.

I finished my shift at 6:00 and went home and watched TV until my new second job started. I showed up at the theater at 2:00 A.M. Dwight was there with his wife pulling a couple of leaf blowers and a vacuum cleaner from the trunk of his car.

We started off by hitting the room that had been subjected to Rocky Horror. Fat rolls of wet toilet paper, chunks of toast and squirt bottles had to be picked up and tossed into the rolling trash barrel. Then we each got a leaf blower going and, starting at the back of the room, blew the trash to the front while walking slowly between the rows of seats. The trash at the front of the room was piled up and deposited in the barrel. Then we mopped. Normally, we would only spot mop, but after Rocky Horror, a thorough cleansing was necessary. The one room took about three hours to clean. We moved to the other one, which went much faster. When it was done, Dwight brought me over to the supply closet.

"Me and the manager are the only ones with keys to this closet," he said gravely. "If you need anything from the closet, ask ME. I will come and open it for you." Dwight, cleaner of movie theaters and holder of the supply closet key, was clearly proud of his lofty position.

We moved on to the men's bathroom. Here, the toilets were scrubbed out, the mirrors cleaned, the floor swept and mopped and the trash emptied. Simple and painless. When we hit the ladies crapper, Dwight pointed me over to a metal box screwed onto the side of the first stall partition.

"Ya gotta clean out the rag box every day," he said.

It was about eight in the morning. I was tired and slightly brain dead, but not so much that I didn't approach the shiny metal box with a certain degree of apprehension.

I inserted the key into the locked box and opened it. It was indeed a rag box in the truest sense of the term and I couldn't help wondering why in god's name anyone would see a need to put a lock on this thing. I would've sold my ass for a pair of rubber gloves. Instead, I settled for a big wad of toilet paper, using it to pull the offending tampons and napkins out of the box. Some were stuck to the sides and I had to push and pull to scrape them off. I felt a vague urge to vomit. I cleaned two more rag boxes while Dwight stood by chuckling. Apparently he saw the situation as being a form of custodial hazing.

The bathrooms cleaned, Dwight ushered me around emptying the trash. We tossed it all in the dumpster on the side of the building and headed off for the other theater while Mary stayed on to vacuum the lobby.

The other theater was more of the same, though not quite as bad; there were four screens, but the rooms were smaller and there was no Rocky Horror. The lobby was smaller but the bathrooms were bigger, particularly the men's. But the job only took a few hours.

When we were finishing the last room, I found a five-dollar bill on the floor. Dwight quickly grabbed it and gave me $2.50 change.

"Any money we find, we split," he said sternly.

I'd been picking up loose change all night but I figured I'd earned it before the sharing rule had been brought to my attention, so I saw no need to split my findings.

By 11:30 we were back at the first theater. Mary was sitting on the plush lobby bench. Dwight and I hustled to put the cleaning supplies away and we left just as the theater employees were arriving.

It only took a few days for Dwight to leave me on my own. Mary stopped helping with the cleaning and Dwight and I worked on different parts of the theaters, which left me a lot of time for daydreaming.

I was usually already at the theater, waiting, when Dwight showed up, his massive key chain dangling from the belt around his skinny hips. He looked to be about my age and was in fact only a couple of years older than me. He was from Wisconsin, which explained his decision to marry and have a kid at such a young age. His appearance was that of a goofy, gawky teenaged kid, and no matter how hard he tried to look the part — and he tried like hell — he just didn't exude a janitorial air.

As harmless as he looked, he was a little prick. Having someone to boss around obviously brought him great joy and when he saw I was a good, fast worker, he immediately began taking advantage of the opportunities my reliability afforded.

Dwight liked to start early, so on weekdays we were at the first theater by 7:30. Since the theaters were far less populated during the week, the job went more quickly and we were usually done by noon. At first, the only key I was allowed to touch was the one used to open the rag boxes. But soon, Dwight started leaving me alone at the theater with the keys to the lobby doors and supply closets, claiming he had to take his wife to the doctor. Within a couple of weeks she was going to the doctor just about every day. I knew damn well that Dwight was grossing $800 a week for cleaning both theaters and he was only paying me $250 a week under the table. He was turning a tidy profit while I was doing most of the work. Unless she was experiencing the most difficult pregnancy known to female-kind, the sonofabitch didn't have to take his wife to the doctor every day. He was simply showing up, handing me the keys and — of this I became certain — going back home to bed.

Things deteriorated to the point where I was cleaning the first theater entirely by myself, at which point Dwight would show up and we'd head to the second theater, which was always a breeze. Mary would still sometimes help on weekends, but more often than not, I was left to clean up after the Rocky Horror creeps by myself.

Though I realized I was getting the short end of the stick, I never complained. I much preferred being left alone to do my work; instead of having to listen to Dwight nag me WHILE I was working, he'd come in after I'd finished and get all flustered about the things I hadn't done according to his stringent custodial guidelines.

On my own, I rather enjoyed cranking up the leaf blower and effortlessly pushing the empty popcorn buckets, soda cups and crushed Raisinet boxes down in front of the screen. Since Dwight was seldom around to check that I'd done a thorough mopping (a mandatory chore once a week), I stuck with spot mopping; by the time he showed up, everything was already dry so he had no way of knowing whether or not I'd done the unnecessary job. Since the house lights were dim, I'd occasionally forgo the mopping for a nice, long cigarette break, secure in the knowledge that no matter how hard the little fucker looked, it would still be tough for him to find a spot I'd missed. He usually found something anyway, but hey, I was just a dim-witted janitor's assistant.

I played dumb from the get-go. Though Dwight was intellectually challenged — if not impaired — I still managed to act more stupid than him. I quickly took advantage of the image I'd cultivated: a not-too-bright stooge, but a hard worker; a guy who tries his best but just can't help occasionally forgetting to clean the mirrors or scrape out the rag boxes.

Also, on my own I was able to net a nice little pocketful of tips every day courtesy of sloppy theater patrons. Mostly I found change, but a few days a week I'd hit a crumpled pile of singles or a stray ten spot. Once, when Dwight was cleaning the room next to mine up in Deerfield, I found a wallet. I opened it up and discovered a $100 bill inside. I quickly pocketed the dough and stashed the wallet under the seat. When Dwight found it the next day he was disappointed indeed to find that it contained no cash. "What we find, we split," was so much bullshit. Dwight never once gave me a dime and after my first day, I never gave him anything either. I started coming to work with loose change in my pocket so he couldn't accuse me of holding out. Every once in a while he'd ask, but I always gave him the good old bewildered look. Sorry Dwight, I guess I'm just not a lucky guy.

The theater in Deerfield was patronized by the upper middle class people of that area, so silver and green fringe benefits were much more common there. So, for some reason, were empty beer bottles. Every day I'd end up with a case of empties in my trash barrel. Occasionally I'd run across a couple of unopened beers, warm yet invariably of a higher quality than I was used to: St. Pauli Girl, Heineken, Beck's. It was tough to smuggle those out so I always ended up sharing.

So here I was working as a janitor seven days a week, and four more days a week as a theater employee in addition to going to school four nights a week. Everyone at the theater had to work one weekend night and one weekend day. Therefore, every Saturday and Sunday I was faced with fourteen-hour days, my only consolation being money — which at that point in my life was still enough to keep me going.

My career as a janitor came to a close due to several factors. First, the Corporate President in Charge of Making Employees' Lives Miserable decided that the scuffmarks on the backs of the seats had to be cleaned more frequently than we were doing it. Now once a week I had to scrub the hell out of all the seats with a rag and a bottle of semi-toxic fluid. Instead of ending my Wednesday at noon, I was stuck there until three. If that wasn't bad enough, Dwight, fully realizing the potential to utilize me to further his own brown-nosing, stepped up his gum-scraping efforts. This resulted in me sitting on the floor of a poorly lit theater with a putty knife attempting to chip petrified gum and soda deposits off of the cement floor. This was getting ridiculous. I was already doing more than half the work, and now this butthole was getting in better with the boss at my expense.

I began to be more careful about emptying my cigarette butts into the garbage so that Dwight would never know how much time I spent lounging around on the lobby benches thinking about more important things than dirty toilets and mops. I began to spend so much time just sitting around that I seemed to be working much slower. Dwight must've caught on because he tried to bust me several times by popping in unexpectedly in hopes of finding me laying on the bench. However, there was a small space between the curtains, which provided me with the perfect vista for spotting Dwight's car zipping across the empty mall parking lot a good two minutes before he was in the door. He almost caught me late one morning by taking a different route — he came from the opposite direction, around a corner. Unfortunately for him, he had come too late; I'd finished everything but the vacuuming. When he walked in I was sitting on the bench finishing my cigarette. He looked triumphant.

"How much more is there to do?" he asked, glancing at his watch.

"Just the vacuuming," I said. He kept the vacuum cleaner in the trunk of his car.

His victory cruelly snatched away, he went outside, grabbed the vacuum and ran it furiously over the carpet.

After that he started getting snippy with me, which just made me slack off even more. I finally gave him two weeks notice, a process I was never fond of but one I knew would be best considering I'd be running into him on weekends when I was working the early shift on the door or behind the counter. After I quit, he made a snide comment about my inability to handle tough work. I just laughed like he had hit upon one of the great truths in life.

A few months later, he and his wife moved up to Wisconsin where they'd gotten a couple of cleaning contracts. The cheeseheads always end up going back to the land of the dead. When I heard the contracts were open, I briefly considered trying to get them, but I was leery of working seven days a week, 365 days a year for GCC, one of the stingiest, nastiest corporations ever to exist. Before I had a chance to make up my mind, they hired a couple of Polish ladies. Just as well. I would've fucked the whole thing up anyway.

THE PIZZA BOY

I was thirteen years old when I got my first job. I really wasn't prepared. I was still early in my career as a juvenile delinquent and while minor, petty theft helped to pay for my smoking habit, cold hard cash was needed for many of the necessities, like pot, beer and heavy metal records. I lived in Prospect Heights, Illinois, a small town which was well on its way to becoming a full-fledged suburb. One might think that my life would have been easier had I simply asked my parents for money. Oh, that I could, but my parents were truly middle class both in terms of their income and their values. My parents' children were never given money. We were taught to work for a living.

I'd never really done much work before that. The Whelan brothers worked as caddies at Rolling Green Country Club and my parents thought that would be a good job for me, but I wasn't about to get up at 4:30 a.m. to go rushing off to the caddyshack. When I was 12, I'd worked for one day with the Whelan brothers for their father — a landscaper. I thought it would be cool to work all day and get paid real money. We spent nine hours wandering around the grounds of a new condo complex on Lake Street in Glenview picking up rocks and tossing them in buckets. Every once in a while, their old man would come by and yell at us to move faster. I could never understand what the hell he was saying because of his thick Irish accent, but I knew he thought of us — well, me — as a lazy, work-evading twelve-year-old stooge. At the end of the workday, I was reluctantly given a five-dollar bill for my troubles. I walked away feeling screwed; so what if we'd spent most of the day fucking around? That was no reason to give us a five-dollar slap in the face. Strangely, his youngest son Tom, with whom I was goofing off, ended up taking over the business. I believe he still runs it; a couple of years ago I read an interview with him in the *Sun-Times* regarding the work ethic of Mexicans. I hope he's not still spending his days throwing rocks at the side of buildings and the occasional car instead of dutifully placing them into buckets.

My first real boss also had a thick accent, but his was Italian. His name was Pete, also known as Pete Primo because he owned the two Pete's-A-Primo pizza joints in Mt. Prospect and Prospect Heights. My sister's boyfriend had a gig at the Prospect Heights Primo's and told me that if I was polite and dressed nice, I could meet Pete Primo and probably get a gig washing dishes.

The Mt. Prospect Primo's had no restaurant; it was strictly delivery and carry out. The Prospect Heights Primo's was an actual restaurant, and it was there I went to apply for my first job with the almost-mythical Pete Primo. Mitch, my sister's boyfriend, came out from the kitchen and told me to wait in a booth until Pete Primo showed up. He gave me a basket of fries and I sat there munching happily until Pete arrived. I couldn't tell you how old he was — he could've been thirty or he could have been fifty. He was only as tall as me and he had a face that looked like it had done time in a few boxing rings. After checking out the kitchen, he came over and sat down across from me.

My interview went fairly smoothly, though Pete's accent caused me to ask him to repeat just about every question he asked. After ascertaining that I had my parents' permission to work, he told me the gig was mine and I should start immediately.

Mitch brought me back behind the kitchen where the dirty dishes were already stacked up next to the sinks. I started in and kept going until 9:00. Every once in a while one of the waitresses would come back and ask me to re-wash a dish or something, but I caught on pretty quick. By the end of my shift, Pete and Mitch were watching me whip through a pile of dishes with satisfied looks on their faces.

"He's faster than Rocky," Pete remarked. I was bashfully pleased at hearing this praise, but at the same time, I felt a bit like a dog that had just taken its first shit outside the house instead of on the living room rug.

My parents were pleased that I was working, especially my father. I received a stern warning not to let the job interfere with school, and not to slack off on my duties around the house — cutting grass, taking out the trash, shoveling snow, and doing whatever crazy jobs my father would think up for me every Saturday, which could range from relatively painless chores like changing the license plates on the Matador when the new ones came in, to twisted exercises in father-son bonding through pointless labor like helping him build a bin to hold firewood.

I was well liked at Pete's-A-Primo. I was the little kid who took his job very seriously. And why not? I figured a couple more years of this and I could work my way up to cook, at which point I'd drop out of school, buy a van with a stereo system and waterbed in the back and smoke pot every night with slutty girls who had feathered hair. My apartment would be filled with sound-activated lights that would pulsate crazily while the Alice Cooper and Judas Priest records were cranking out on the stereo. The walls would be covered in black light posters and mirrors with bootlegged logos of bands like Black Sabbath. I could make a little extra money dealing pot on the side. And I'd go back to my old school and tell my teachers to fuck off, and finally beat the shit out of my dad.

It was a well-conceived plan, but I hadn't figured on learning to despise work so quickly. That I was well liked was fine. In slow moments, I'd sweep the restaurant, occasionally breaking into a broom guitar solo to the delight of my co-workers who surely knew that I had no idea how foolish I looked. I got along well with Mitch and Ron. Ron was the main cook. He had long hair and his own apartment and he spoke in code with Mitch. "10-4" was easy enough to understand, as was a "Big 10-4," but a "Big 10-4 V.R." was beyond my comprehension. The infamous "Helmut Buff" had me slightly baffled until I took into account the occurrence of the utterance in relation to the proximity of attractive females.

Pete had mentioned that I was faster than Rocky, the surly twenty-one-year-old burnout who washed dishes on the day shift. I found this remarkable as practically every evening I was confronted by angry waitresses demanding silverware, at which point I would sigh and drag the bucket of unwashed silverware from under the sink, where Rocky liked to hide it. How could I be faster than a guy who stashed half of his work for my later enjoyment? Not that the remnants of somebody else's job not done was the worst thing under the sink. Not by far. That honor would go to The Trap. I imagine that cleaning up the remains of suicides or shoveling shit must be worse jobs than cleaning The Trap in the sink of an Italian restaurant, but for me, The Trap was a living hell. The smell was enough to drive any sane man from the depths of the rear kitchen. Scraping the gunk and slime out with one's hands was a job most people would trade for a gig as the night janitor in a Greyhound station men's room. Rocky never cleaned the trap, so it always ended up as my job. I did it scowling, cussing, whining and taking frequent breaks to avoid vomiting.

Washing dishes, playing broom guitar, cleaning The Trap, and occasionally getting the honor of making a salad, all for below minimum wage, got old in about three days. I was constantly tired and I worked on weekend nights, which interfered enormously with my advancement in the ranks of the northwest suburbs' social outcasts.

There were good moments; whenever Pete Primo's wife — a pretty, petite brunette — came in, she always talked to me, giving me an up-close view of hidden breasts and delicious curves underneath her blue jeans. And the con-artist debacle was minor fun. That involved a woman who had eaten nine-tenths of a plate of linguini before shrieking that there was a cigarette butt in her food. Pete Primo rushed out to apologize, assuring the woman that she wouldn't have to pay, and that she could come back for a free meal any time. Ron picked up the nearly empty plate of pasta and peered at it skeptically.

"Hey Pete," he said.

"Wha? Wha' is it?" Pete was flustered and in no mood for contrary evidence. Everyone else in the restaurant was either staring at the scene or inspecting his own food. This was a potential disaster and Pete wanted nothing more than to get the woman out of there. Ron held his tongue. But after she'd left, Ron took Pete back to kitchen and showed him the plate.

"Look at that," he said. "She ate the food and put her own cigarette out in it to get a free meal."

"No, no," said Pete. "Somebody back here been smokin' and I wanna know WHO!"

"Pete, look at the butt. We all smoke Marlboros with a brown filter. I don't even know what kind of cigarette this is — Refrigerator Lights or something. And she had a pack of 'em right on the table."

"Well," sniffed an obviously hurt Pete, "No free meal for her if she come back!" Then, to nobody in particular: "Why somebody wanna do somethin' like that? And a *woman*! I work so hard to be stolen from?" And on and on. When Pete got on his hard-working man rant you just had to leave the room. Spit flew from his mouth, and his face got all red, but mostly you left because it was so embarrassing; for all his bluster he was just having a big temper tantrum. Whining louder and louder in his broken English, letting all the employees (and even the deafest of patrons) know that we were essentially a bunch of lazy, overpaid jackoffs who were lucky to even have a job working in his restaurant. If you left the room, you didn't have to work so hard to conceal your laugh.

Two weeks into the gig I was getting set to go out riding with the Whelan brothers on their new RM-80. An afternoon of tearing around the maze of trails and trying to outrace the cops when they made their inevitable appearance was shattered when my mother informed me that I had to work. I called Pete Primo at the restaurant.

"I'm not coming in," I said. "I quit."

"Wha'? Why?"

"I hate it. I'm tired all the time and I can't stand it."

"You quit in two weeks," he said.

"Nope. I quit now."

"You can' leave your employer without giving two week notice!"

"Sorry," I said. "I quit." I hung up to the sound of Joe yelling about two weeks. My mother gave me a stern lecture, which I blissfully ignored. Then I headed out to the field behind the house to burn rubber.

That wasn't the end of my career in the Italian food service industry. A friend got me a job at a Domino's Pizza in Elk Grove Village when I was twenty, broke and in need of any kind of gig. I quickly learned — though sadly, not for the last time — that there is no such thing as a friend getting you a job. If a friend ever offers to get you a job, forget his phone number and avoid him on the street because he is no friend.

Working for Domino's might not have been so bad if it weren't for the hat and the nametag. Any job that forces you to wear a hat and a nametag is demeaning. It is a uniform designed to make you feel subservient and helpless the second you start working there. They put you in a silly costume — always with garish colors and 1976 fashion designs — so you know your place. I stole as much money as I could from the shit hole before quitting after three weeks.

I ended up back at Primo's when I was twenty-one. I had applied for a delivery job at the Mt. Prospect location — the Prospect Heights restaurant had gone under several years earlier. Apparently, Pete Primo nearly had a heart attack when he saw my name on the application.

Some months later, I was out in Palatine for some reason and stopped by the third and newest Primo's in the strip mall. Don, Mitch's younger brother, owned half of the Palatine location; Pete owned the other half. I asked Don for a gig. He didn't have much for me but agreed to let me make deliveries during lunchtime; Pete seldom came by, but he always showed up in the evenings. The consequences of my employment wouldn't be devastating, but why would poor Don want to put up with a livid Pete if it could be avoided?

Don worked insane hours. He was there all day, seven days a week. I'd heard him talk about other employees but I never saw one. They showed up when they felt like it, which was seldom, and Don let them get away with it because he had no other choice. Often I stayed longer than I needed to, waiting for the odd delivery to come in so I could pick up a few precious extra bucks. I'd hang around talking with Don and watching ball games on the TV in the kitchen.

Most of my deliveries were to offices. People who work in offices are the cheapest, stingiest tippers in the world. Delivering three pizzas and receiving a fifty-cent tip does not induce you to be extra careful in making sure the jerk's next meal doesn't end up hitting the ground a few times before it arrives in his ungrateful hands.

But I was happy to be making anything and Don was a good boss. He knew I was broke and living in a punk house. He gave me as much work as he could and he always fed me and sent me home with a couple of slices of pizza. Pete's-A-Primo pizza was deservedly renowned in the northwest suburbs, and still is, I assume. I've never eaten a pizza with a better crust, and what's inside is just perfection. I've seen the pizzas made many times. I know what the ingredients are. I make a pretty good home-cooked pizza myself, but I've never been able to come close to duplicating a Primo pizza. To his credit, Pete Primo was no dummy. After the Prospect Heights restaurant failed, he went back to making pizzas for take-out and delivery in small storefronts; his pizza was his golden goose and he didn't screw around with it. Pete didn't make a thin crust pizza. He made pizza one way, and if you didn't like it, he sincerely thought you were a complete idiot. Most people were smart enough to appreciate it.

The gig only lasted a couple of months until my car was smashed while parked on North Avenue by a drunk named Jesus, and Don finally sold his share in the Palatine Primo's and took a less stressful job. But the next time I'm up there I might stop in for a slice. I'll just have to make sure Pete's not around first.

THE LIBRARY AIDE

After my car was totaled while parked innocently next to a meter on North Avenue, I lost all hope of decent employment. Though I hadn't been making big money delivering pizzas, it had been enough to pay the rent on the room I was living in at the loft in Wicker Park, particularly when augmented with the landscaping work Jughead and I had been doing with a friend twice a week. I had been on the verge of signing a lease on an apartment of my own when a drunk named Jesus demolished the faithful '76 Chevy Malibu that had gotten me to and from many jobs. Defeated, I moved back in with my parents. There was, however, a slight snag. My parents had moved to Wisconsin.

Though the thought of living in this country's most singularly frightening state caused me no small amount of physical and emotional discomfort, I was without a choice. In October of 1989, I moved to Wisconsin. By the time a year had passed, I was becoming desperate. My parents didn't seem to mind me living in their home, but my predilection for quitting jobs after I had served what I considered to be a respectable three months quite obviously annoyed them. They began needling me about my future. And, as is wont to happen when forced to live with your parents, their needling began affecting me in a disturbing way; I, too became concerned about my future. What was I doing fucking around with a nowhere band, writing things nobody would ever read? I needed a purpose in life. The reality of the world of journalism began to seep into my brain; there was no way I would ever get a gig as a paying writer without getting some sort of degree in a field that I knew little about, aside from the dreaded Inverted Pyramid Principle, the very thought of which disgusted me.

But since I was bound to be drifting about, working a succession of lousy jobs for the rest of my miserable life, I figured it wouldn't be all that painful to return to school and attempt to get an Associate's Degree in something. At least I'd be able to make enough money to support myself should I ever tire of hopping from one dreadful job to the next. My field of endeavor would be drug and alcohol counseling. There was a good job market for someone with these skills and it was a subject I felt I knew a bit about, having been analyzed by many a drug counselor myself.

Lacking both the grades and finances for a four-year institution, I committed to continuing my education at community college. After no small amount of mental hand wringing brought on by painful memories of my previous thirteen-year firewalk through various schools, I signed up for four classes at Waukesha County Technical College. Though I failed miserably in my attempts to get financial aid, that didn't stop the old man from winning the $400 for tuition and books in a poker game. I had a purpose. As a plus, my parents would be off my back. Almost.

After a week and a half of school, the pressure began again to get a job. This was really too much. I was in school already and now they wanted me to get a job as well! When would the insanity end? I put it off as long as possible and finally, after being prodded one time too many, I glanced at the bulletin board in the Science building. The library was hiring.

Oh, the library. I had spent many days at the local library as a child. It had nothing but positive connotations for me. Peaceful, quiet, laid back. This was the job for me.

I strode purposefully to the den of the written word, located at the northwest end of the campus. Once inside, I asked the student at the desk for an application. A woman of about 55, smiling and teetering slightly, came out from behind the partition and sat me down. She shook my hand and produced a pen and the requisite forms, introducing herself as Betty.

I filled out the application under her watchful gaze as she adjusted and readjusted her glasses. My, she looked pleased to have an applicant for the position of library aide! I submitted the forms with as much of a smile as I could manage to screw up. Betty indicated that she would call me if my application passed the scrutiny of the head librarian, a woman known to me at that point only as Harriet, a name that conjured up an image of a well-fed, mother hen type, stern and demanding on the surface — surely a woman not to be trifled with — but with a heart of gold beating steadily underneath her sensible support bra.

I practically skipped home, secure in the knowledge that the mere act of filling out an application would subdue my landlords for at least a week. Unfortunately, after three days, I was called back to the library, this time to endure a grueling interview session with the famed Harriet. My mental picture of her was fairly accurate, but if a heart of gold indeed pounded beneath her formidable bosom, it beat for persons other than potential library aides. As she shook my hand and ushered me out to meet my supervisor, I could see that it pained her to smile at me as much as it did me to smile back.

Though the kind if somewhat bumbling Betty was to be my supervisor, she had, sometime between the time of my application and subsequent hiring, suffered a heart attack. In her place, a pleasantly thin, fifty-ish woman named Gladys was engaged to verse me in the skills required of a student employee of the WCTC library. Gladys was cheery and peppy, the type of personality that generally causes feelings of black hatred in me, particularly when the possessor of said attitude is a co-worker. I was soon to learn that the effervescent Gladys was hardly a model of employee perfection. Raised in a different time than I, she naturally had her own methods for expressing her feelings about the job, but it quickly became clear to me that she had at least a touch of the anti-work virus that so ravaged my own soul.

I picked my own hours and was assured that they could be switched easily if I gave reasonable notice. I would work four hours shifts Monday through Thursday and a full eight-hour shift on Friday. My duties included checking books out, cleaning out the return bin and checking the books back in, organizing books on the shelves, organizing the periodicals in the stacks behind the desk, general cleaning and organizing of the main section of the library, putting covers and cards in the new books and any other tasks that might come up during the course of a shift.

Upon arriving at the library, I walked to the back of the periodical stacks behind the front desk and wrote in my time of arrival on my shift sheet. I'd then pin my nametag prominently on my shirt above my left breast and check my time sheet box for my list of duties for the day.

I was soon settled into a routine. If I started my shift in the morning, I'd usually grab the books and magazines from the return bin and check them back in, placing the cards back in the pockets and carting them back behind the desk. I'd then organize the books according to the Library of Congress system, wheel the carts out and replace the books on the shelves.

Once a week, I would clean the computer screens and keyboards that functioned as our card catalog. Other mornings, I'd organize the reserve books and do mailings; we often had requests from other libraries for books and I was invariably charged by Gladys to take the beaten up, fifty times recycled mailing envelopes, stuff them with the proper books, fill out the mailing labels on the IBM electric typewriter, staple and tape the packages and toss them onto the outgoing mail cart.

I started work at eight A.M. and took my first break around 10:00. I'd pull on my leather jacket and scarf and huddle outside the library entrance smoking cigarettes until my fifteen minutes were up. If I was working an eight-hour shift, I'd take lunch at 12:00 or 12:30. I'd spend the first fifteen minutes wolfing down a couple of sandwiches and reading the *Chicago Tribune*. Then I'd bundle up and chain-smoke three cigarettes in my remaining fifteen minutes outside the library doors.

Afternoons were a bit more relaxed. Harriet tended to take long lunches so there was less pressure and there was invariably less work to do. Sometimes I would find myself thrust into the back corner with the aged Violet whose job duties totally mystified me; she never moved from her table and never seemed to be doing much of anything. I'd put slipcovers on new books, type up cards for them and paste the cards in the front. Then I'd ink up the WCTC stamp, hit the front and the middle of the book, and place it on the cart to hit the shelves. This was one aspect of the job at which I was totally hopeless. I'd pick the wrong size slipcover and end up with a wrinkly mess. I'd stick the card in on the wrong spot. I'd stamp the wrong pages. After a few abortive attempts, the ladies seemed to understand that I wasn't cut out for the job.

Around 4:00, Carol came in. Carol was exclusively in charge of periodicals and I was her favorite cohort. The youngest of the library ladies, she was a forty-ish woman who took her duties seriously but had an impish streak; often she was given to sarcastic, catty remarks about the other employees — especially Harriet — particularly when in the company of Gladys. After several weeks of careful whispering, the ladies realized that I was no rat and stopped trying to hide their semi-subversive dialogues from my tender ears. I rather enjoyed their caustic commentary; if an obnoxious patron annoyed them, they would roll their eyes and occasionally whisper such insults as "What a crank!" under their breath, casting furtive glances to make sure none but yours truly was within earshot. On one memorable occasion, after a stressful staff meeting with Harriet, Gladys, her eyes filled with hate, whispered, "Bitch!" in a strangled voice. I was duly impressed and nodded my head in agreement.

I'm certain that there were many more vitriolic exchanges between the two but I had my duties. When Carol came in, I started my work for her. First and foremost was the updating of the periodical section. Our magazines went back ten years — the most recent five behind the desk and the other five in the stack in the large section upstairs which also featured a huge microfiche section and two career specialists who seemed to spend most of their time elsewhere. My daily task was to chip away at the ongoing job of moving the magazines from six years ago upstairs and then throwing the magazines from eleven years ago away. This was not a one-shift job; in fact, I worked at it for an hour and a half every shift and it took me all semester to finish. Though this job required a certain amount of physical exertion (the magazines could be carted to the stairs but had to be carried up by hand) it was an easy one. The newspapers went back for a year and we kept anywhere from a month to three months' worth behind the desk, depending on the frequency of publication. Once a week, I carted the papers upstairs and threw away the outdated ones.

This was a simple job but Carol expressed admiration for my execution and speed. Clearly, I was the only man for this job. Several times, I attempted to train new employees to assist me, but they invariably grew lazy and screwed up. Within two months, the job was mine and mine alone.

As with every job, I was never late and never left early. I worked hard and seemingly fast, although by this point in my jobs career, I had learned how to drag out a simple task for as long as possible if the next chore was one I'd rather not do. There were many dull moments — straightening chairs and desks in the library, re-stocking pencils and strips of paper at the computer kiosk, replacing microfiche in the huge upstairs library — but even these tasks, though mundane, were simple and appealed to my obsessive nature. In fact, I still think that it was the only job for which I was well suited; almost every task required nothing more than organization skills. Everything went in its place according to a preordained system. Since I am naturally fussy and particular, I took to it like a fish to water.

Still, if my working skills were impeccable, my social skills were anything but. Contrary to my popular image in the punk rock subculture, I suffer from an inherent shyness and social retardation, which makes my exchanges with those outside the subculture clumsy at best. As a result, I keep my mouth shut and my mind on my work. Over the years, this has developed to the point where it demands justification, so I tell myself that I am not interested in dealing with people in a work environment; I am there only because I have to be and anything above and beyond the call of duty is verboten. How much of this is reality and how much of it is self-preservation is a question only a qualified psychologist can answer, but the end result is always the same; I develop tentative, working relationships with my bosses and none whatsoever with my co-workers. I am viewed as an oddball, a weirdo. Sometimes, the verdict is that I'm simply shy. At other times, I'm certain that I'm seen as a mentally unstable criminal. In the case of the library, my image took a beating not only from my co-workers (which wasn't so bad because the turnover rate was incredibly high) but also from my fellow students, patrons of the library. I was the only male in recent history who had lasted more than two days as a library aide. In sub-rural Wisconsin, that immediately must have branded me as a homosexual. I had long hair that hung all over my face. I didn't talk much. I didn't hunt or fish. I wasn't scared of black people. I must've been viewed as a freak.

Although my image made things uncomfortable at times, I was undoubtedly very happy in my job. I could take my time. There were plenty of places to hide when I was supposed to be working. My hours were flexible and if I needed materials from the library for a class, I got them immediately, instead of having to wait around like everyone else. There was really only one awful aspect to the job and that only occurred when there was no other work to do.

I tried to stretch out my daily list as much as possible, but occasionally Harriet would emerge from her office and see me standing around doing nothing. Invariably, I was given the task of organizing the stacks. I never attempted to hide my disgust and frustration with this job, but I never successfully wiggled out of it either. The most I could do was to see it coming and disappear while a less-informed co-worker would be assigned the horrible job.

Books had to be placed in their proper order; library patrons were constantly taking them out and putting them back in the wrong place. They left them on the floor, or piled up in a corner of the shelf. I had to put them back and straighten them out for easy access. I don't quite know why I detested the job so much. Maybe it was because I hated being thrust into the midst of a sea of idiot students. Maybe it was my distaste at having to clean up after slobs. Either way, when given the job, I trudged out as though I was on a death march and slowly, very slowly, went about my task. The technical books section was always a mess. There were huge tomes and skinny little floppy auto repair manuals. After a while, the numbers became a blur. The whole process made me incredibly tired; often I would pull out a stool and lean my head against the stacks for a few moments of rest. If things were busy at the desk, I'd steal away to the magazine stacks upstairs and lie down between the *Ebony*s and the *Popular Mechanics*. I worked in slow motion under the assumption that if this were the one task at which I was a complete failure, the ladies would stop forcing it on me. It never worked.

Conversely, the part of the job I enjoyed the most was replacing the papers and magazines on the shelves. As soon as Carol came in, she'd stamp the new arrivals, zap 'em with the laser that caused the stolen book detector to go off and place them on a cart. I'd stroll out to the magazine racks and replace the daily papers and many of the monthly magazines and journals. I always took my sweet time doing this job. Every periodical was to be placed above its nameplate and things often got screwed up. There were several return sections; when a patron finished with a periodical, he put it back in its pile. The library aides put them back in their proper place. With my stack of magazines and my pad and pencil to mark off the return of the previous month's or day's issue, I was at my best. I was efficient, organized, sleek, a magazine machine. Often, I'd stop to read the latest gossip in *People* or peer at the animal rights ads in *The Progressive*.

After a month at the library, there was only one other student who had been there longer than me — Donna, a seemingly serious-minded woman in her late twenties. She was the EMPLOYEE-WHO-DOES-THE-SAME-SHIT-JOBS-AS-EVERYONE-ELSE-BUT-STILL-ACTS-LIKE-SHE-RUNS-THE-PLACE; there's one at every job. New employees who met her were often confused about her status. Was she a real librarian or merely an aide? She constantly gave orders to the other employees. The first time, I bit. The second time she tried to tell me what to do, I suddenly developed a total hearing loss. After several subsequent attempts to be my boss, she gave up, satisfied with ratting on me to the real librarians. Fortunately, they realized that she was a power freak — an obnoxious blowhard who really didn't know what the hell she was talking about. If she had practiced what she preached, she could have been the thorn in my side that caused me to quit. As it was, she came in late, or not at all, on a constant basis. She always had a mealy mouthed excuse, and the librarians, being kind, forgiving women, accepted them, but they knew the score.

I had settled comfortably into the job when Betty made an unexpected return. Gladys was relived of her duties as boss and went back to her desk working on inter-library loans. Betty barely remembered me, which was understandable given that she had suffered cardiac arrest within hours of hiring me. Though she was gentle and kind, she took no shit either. I soon learned that if I satisfied her criteria as an employee, which simply meant not constantly fucking things up like the other employees, that she would be a powerful ally.

Betty began writing my to-do lists. They were essentially the same as before and, since I kept up my regular pace, no extra work was added. She tried to be stern, but she was a pussycat when it came to taking days off or switching my hours. I was reliable and hardworking in her book, which simply meant that I showed up and did what I was told — golden qualities in a library aide at WCTC.

The only major change caused by Betty's return was that I was immediately trained in desk duty. I checked out books for the patrons. I retrieved reference books for the engineering students and a variety of cassettes detailing the human body for the enormous number of nursing students. I typed and laminated new library cards and entered the information in the computer. I organized the cassettes, videos and reference books. I sent out slips to overdue book borrowers, cleaned out the return bin and made trips upstairs when handed a slip requesting a particularly old periodical. I cleaned the counter and computer screens and organized the cards for books that had been checked out.

The job was generally not too bad, although it did mean direct contact with the public. Soon, however, I learned to take my sweet time in finding what people wanted. If there was a long line, too bad. I hurried for no one, unless Betty or Harriet were around.

Betty sensed that I disliked the job and must have noticed that I wasn't the most cheerful, pleasant employee when forced to deal with the public, so as a result, I usually didn't get more than an hour of desk duty per shift.

I worked two evening shifts a week and soon discovered that 5:00 to 9:30 was the place to be. Harriet and Betty were gone and most of the work for the day was done. The library was quiet and pretty much empty and my bosses were Gladys and Carol. The two ladies really came into their own on the evening shift. They became brazen in their cutting remarks about Harriet and some of the other employees. I was often present during their catty dialogues and it cheered me considerably to listen to them. Watching from a discreet distance, I could see them perched on their stools behind the counter, legs swinging, teeth banging up and down on the Wrigley's, chuckling cynically, bright eyed and slick. I could almost see them thirty years ago. Two semi-tough teenage girls hanging out on the street corner, keeping an eye out for their hoodlum, leather-jacketed boyfriends, cigarettes lodged firmly between heavily-painted lips, swigging from a nameless bottle in a brown paper bag, scaring the hell out of Middle America. These women were cool.

Things went smoothly until the end of the semester. A girl named Diane from my Assessment & Diagnosis class had mentioned that she needed a job. Foolishly, I suggested the library. Though she was the only person in any of my classes who I didn't hate talking to, she was the wrong person to be working with. To be sure, having a co-worker who wasn't a jerk was nice, but she was pretty damn smart and I soon found myself competing with her for the cushy jobs. It was tense at first, but eventually, we settled in and were able to co-exist on a semi-friendly basis.

As the semester came to an end, I decided to stay on for part of the summer until I was to leave on tour with the band. I'd work four eight-hour shifts a week and then say goodbye to the job.

The first two weeks of the summer, the library was closed. Work was hell. All day, I organized the stacks. When the job was finally completed (me and Diane doing the bulk of the work), we were given mind-numbing busy work. The hours dragged by. On my last two days, no one was present but Betty, Diane and myself. Diane and I went through the desks and chairs scrubbing off all the philosophical, hastily scribbled messages to the world like "Fuck" and "EAT SHIT". It was tiring, tedious work, but I knew I was leaving soon. On my last day, I shook hands with Betty, said goodbye to Diane and took one last look at the library I'd never see again. Or so I thought.

Through a set of circumstances I'd rather not go into, I ended up back at WCTC. I'd totally given up the idea of going for a degree in anything, let alone drug and alcohol counseling, which seemed to entail a future of banging your head against a wall, working low paying jobs and following all the rules that made it next to impossible to properly treat someone with an addiction. I was simply biding my time — I had no better plan. I enrolled in four night classes that had nothing to do with my degree and went back to the library.

At first, Betty and Gladys didn't recognize me with my head shaved bald, but soon we were chatting like old friends and I was set up to work Tuesday through Thursday from 9:00-5:30.

As the highest-ranking student aide, I expected a bit of leniency from the ladies, but my tendency to intentionally forget to pin my nametag on my shirt soon drew the attention of a glowering Harriet and I was surreptitiously inspected daily for my identification. The biggest change in the library was the introduction of the computer checkout system. No longer did each patron have to fill out a card — the book was scanned into the computer with his or her library card. However, marking every book in the library was a long process, so we still stuck to our card filing system as well.

Though the day shift was a drag, I soon developed my old rhythm. I was given the same jobs on the same days and I learned how to drag them out so that I wouldn't have to do busy work. Cigarette breaks had become more pleasant at the end of the last semester with the coming of summer, but now fall was here and it was beginning to get ugly and cold again. I worked my shift, finished at 5:30 and ate my sack dinner and went to class. On Thursdays I brought my small traveling bag with me and after my last class ended at 8:40, I was off to my girlfriend's house in Chicago. I'd leave Monday morning and spend the afternoon doing my weekly studying, then head off to class to start the routine again.

While I no longer experienced the tranquility of the evening shift, the day shift got a lot easier when Harriet took her vacation, then a leave of absence to take care of her ill mother. Betty wasn't overjoyed at having to take over Harriet's responsibilities and became a tad cranky, but she had less time to keep an eye out for opportunities to give me extra work. Being the only male employee, the ladies had always exploited me when needed; now they gave me every task that involved lifting, pushing, carting or anything else that involved the slightest physical exertion. I moved large tables by myself; to ask for help meant dealing with two bumbling biddies on the other end who would inevitably cause me to end up with smashed fingers or toes. The set up of the used book sale was entirely my responsibility and I spent a day going up and down stairs carrying armloads of 1,000 page tomes. The bright spot was my retrieval of the table for the sale. Since I've always suffered from a horrible sense of direction and an even worse ability to locate items that are in plain view of everyone else, this one became a true adventure. Through the intricate windings of the basement, up and down stairs, through doors leading to nowhere — it took me hours to find the table and haul it back to the library.

Most memorable was when Gladys gave me the keys to her car and asked me to get the telephone books out of the trunk and deliver them to the cafeteria for the school's recycling drive.

"It's a brown Buick, license plate BRV 270, and it's near the back of the west parking lot."

I bundled up and trudged out to the lot. I looked for brown cars. None. I tried the three other parking lots. Nothing. I went back and looked for Buicks. Hey! There it was! A brown Buick, right at the end of the row. I hustled down. Wrong license number. Again, I made a semi-thorough check. No luck. I walked up the path back to the library and reported my lack of success to a frowning Gladys. Again she explained where the car was, taking me over to the window and pointing at the lot. Again she gave me the license number. She clenched her teeth as I grabbed a slip of paper and wrote it down.

I lit a cigarette as I left the library and sauntered down to the lot. Christ, it was getting cold. I couldn't go wrong now, though. I had the make, model, color and license number. I walked a little slower, savoring the cigarette. I reached the lot and began my search again. No luck. I was beginning to get strange looks from the people coming in and out of the lot. I went to the other lots and checked. Nothing. Now I was starting to get a little worried. I didn't give a crap about the telephone books. Hell, getting phone books from Gladys' car was not exactly part of my job description. But I was feeling stupid, and I knew that if I went back to the library empty handed, the ladies' opinion of me would go from a hardworking, yet somewhat flaky oddball to a mentally incompetent simpleton. I started at the first lot and walked slowly between the cars, checking each license plate carefully. I knew it was stupid to be inspecting a green Jeep Cherokee, but I did anyway, just to set my mind at ease. I had just gone down the first row when it started snowing. By the time I'd meticulously inspected each car in the first lot, huge, wet flakes were standing an inch deep on the ground. I pulled my scarf tighter and moved on to the second lot. Then the third, fourth and fifth. That fucking car was nowhere to be found. But I wasn't going to give up. The snow was really coming down now and I had to scrunch over to read some of the plates. When I had made my way through all the cars again, I lit another cigarette and wondered if I was finally losing my mind. I checked behind the cafeteria, library and science building, where some of the employees parked their cars. Nothing even resembling a brown Buick. I swatted the ice off my scarf and walked slowly back to the library. When Gladys saw me, she smiled brightly.

"Sure took you long enough!"

"Well, I hate to tell you this Gladys, but I just can't find your car."

Amusement turned to disgust. I was a worm at the foot of a powerful, superior specimen of humanity. Muttering, Gladys pulled on her coat and sped out of the library with me on her heels. I didn't dare light up a cigarette this time. We practically ran down the hill, into the second row of cars, third car from the back.

"It's right HERE!"

How the fuck did I miss it? Subconscious passive-aggression? Sheer idiocy? Temporary frontal lobotomy? I was a beaten man as Gladys opened the trunk, loaded my arms with phone books and hustled back to the library. I dropped the books off in the cafeteria and was about to light a butt for the walk back when I noticed Gladys squinting at me suspiciously through the library window. I stepped up my pace and went back in.

I was soon forgiven, though I was doubtless the subject of derision by Gladys and Carol that evening. Still, things were back to normal soon enough, though I noticed that Gladys made a point of getting anyone but me to run errands that required leaving the library.

The end was anticlimactic. The semester ended and I served out two weeks of duty over winter vacation before filling out my last timesheet. As I said goodbye to the ladies for the last time, I tried to remember the good times. Memories of the ups and downs of my days at the library filled my mind. Who would be the man of the house? Certainly not Walter, a recent addition who wore hearing aids and needed a cane to walk. He wasn't physically able, the poor guy. Worse yet, he was lazy, and his breathing was so labored it could be heard from 200 yards away which meant he couldn't successfully hide out. Lazy is fine — lazy and obvious is not. Many was the time a disgusted librarian would find the spottily-bearded Walter lying on his side in the middle of an aisle like a grotesque Playgirl pin-up, ostensibly organizing the stacks. Gladys developed the disturbing habit of creeping up on the poor bastard and hissing "WALTER!" at him as if she'd just caught him jacking off. At least she had something to keep her amused. Carol would have to find someone else to continue the endless rotation of periodicals. I almost felt sorry for her. Surely she knew her hopes for finding a worker who even came close to my own levels of speed and accuracy were slight indeed. Betty took my departure in stride, wishing me well and giving my hand a firm shake. Diane wished me luck with my band and even Violet crept out from the back to bid me farewell. Last was Harriet. She came out of her office, towering above me, her matronly bosom jutting forth seriously. She smiled as she shook my hand, a smile apparently reserved for greeting new employees and seeing them off into the harsh world.

The library ladies would go on without me. Sure, I might have been a bit flaky in their eyes, but I was dependable and hardworking. I was a rock. I was the consummate library aide, the likes of which they'd never see again. I imagined them in ten years, still mourning the loss of the finest aide ever to grace their presence. I looked back at the library one last time as I walked away. Then I pulled out a cigarette, lit it, and felt around in my jacket pocket for the cool bottle opener I'd swiped on my last day.

WE STAND ON GUARD FROM THEE

We crossed the border in the wee hours of the morning of October 18, 1995 to start the Canadian leg of the tour opening for Green Day. By the time we settled into the Vancouver hotel, we were already aware of the upcoming referendum. As we traveled across Canada, from Vancouver to the Edmonton Coliseum, the Saddledome in Calgary, the Agridome in Regina and Winnipeg Arena (with its hideous, oversized portrait of the queen hanging from the rafters, glaring at us as we played our set, transfixing us with its ugliness, mesmerizing us with its audacity, sending out what we only hoped was an incorrect message that the residents of the greater Winnipeg area were nothing more than a bunch of mush-minded sycophants), we became more and more aware of the importance of the referendum to most Canadians. If the French-Canadian separatists got their way, perhaps the Canadian government would finally rid themselves of the age-old liberal dilemma of treating seriously the political temper tantrums and ridiculous demands of anyone who paints themselves as oppressed. Maybe the country would see an end to highway signs sporting messages in both English and French, even in such unlikely places as Vulcan, Alberta and Eyebrow, Saskatchewan. Perhaps they could concentrate on getting some four-lane inter-province highways into places other than Quebec and Ontario. Hell, they could finally get around to dropping the metric system.

The people we met who saw it in political terms — those lefties who would normally side with anyone perceived as an underdog — instead asserted that the real issue wasn't the Quebecers' sovereignty but rather the plight of Quebec natives (the Canadian version of American Indians). The other Canadians we met weren't filled with hatred for Quebecers — instead, in their uniquely Canadian way, they seemed to view the separatists like they would the cranky old guy down the street who won't give your ball back when it gets knocked into his yard — a minor nuisance perhaps, but not worthy of getting yourself all worked up (then again, Canadians don't get all worked up about anything except beer, hockey and donuts, in that order).

Quebecers, we were finding, didn't really have anybody's sympathy. They'd bullied the government into making Canada a bilingual nation. They were considered to be even more obnoxious than the real French. They were a province full of snobs who would like nothing more than to cut the hyphenated "Canadian" away from their nationality like a surgeon lancing a boil. Yes, they call themselves French, but they know that the rest of the world calls them French-Canadian, and it hurts.

By the time we reached Edmonton, I'd decided that the Quebecers didn't really want to separate from the rest of Canada; they were just trying to get attention as they do about once every ten years. Many Canadians, however, weren't convinced. The general feeling was that it was going to be a close vote (I couldn't argue with that) and that it could go either way (I could argue with that). Clinton had already made vague threats to cut off American support if Quebec went independent; the border problems that would ensue would be a nightmare. Losing federal funds alone would cause bedlam, riots and mad rushes to cross the border. Without full cooperation from the Canadian and American governments, an independent Quebec would turn into a third world country quicker than you can say frog legs.

Naturally, though I knew better, I truly hoped the separatists would win.

We moved on to Maple Leaf Gardens in Toronto, the Sudbury Arena (where the OHL's Sudbury Wolves play), and finally to the Forum in Montreal.

The first thing I noticed as we entered Quebec was that, unlike the rest of Canada, there wasn't a Tim Horton's (Tim Horton's is a chain of donut shops — featuring some of the best coffee available north of the border — named after the former Maple Leafs and Sabres player who died in a car crash over 25 years ago) or Robin's Donuts every 10 feet. Or meters. The second thing I noticed was that the signs were not bilingual like the rest of Canada — they were only in French. Typical. The third thing I noticed came about when we met Ghislaine, the woman who would be promoting the shows in Montreal, Quebec City, Ottawa, Halifax and Fredricton. My wife, who was our tour manager, introduced herself to Ghislaine.

"Oh, your name is Portia," she said.

"Yes," answered Portia, preparing for the usual spiel to explain her name. "It's from Shakespeare."

"Ah, I am sorry I do not know that," said Ghislaine. "I am French, you see. French schools do not teach Shakespeare."

French?!?!??

"She's not French," I told Portia later. "She's a fucking Canadian. She has maple syrup coursing through her veins. She was raised on a diet of donuts and Molson. She knows Maurice Richard's stats like Bob Costas knows Mickey Mantle's! She buys her hockey tickets with easily-tearable money that has the faces of British royalty on it and the only thing that she has in common with the French is that they both measure distance in kilometers."

I began to see the main difference between the French and the French-Canadians. While it's true that the French are generally arrogant and irritating, the country is not the stereotype you see in the movies. After visiting France, my impression is that the French arrogance is based on a superiority complex whereas the French-Canadian arrogance is based on an inferiority complex. The dumb bastards want so bad to be French they can taste it, but at best, they're gutter French. My guess is that the French see their Canadian counterparts as unworthy pretenders to the throne.

(By the way, France was the only European country I visited in which penises in smut mags are covered with black bars [I bought a smut mag in every European country I visited in 1995 — for research purposes, of course]. When I entered a sex shop in Paris and mentioned to the shopkeeper that he wanted too much for a piece of lingerie [figuring that being on tour in a band would probably be the only chance I'd ever have to get to Paris, I simply had to buy lingerie for the wife. Chicks love that romantic nonsense...], my assertion did not offend him in the least. In fact we bargained until the price was satisfactory. He even threw in a cock ring. Point is, he didn't treat me like a no-class American pig [even though I was kind of striving for that effect]. Okay, so I only spent two days in France. I only spent two days in Quebec. So what. I'm an American — I'm allowed to make snap judgments.)

We left the Longueuil hotel in the late morning for the three-hour drive to Quebec City. We made a quick stop at a Burger King and somehow managed to walk away with fries and sandwiches even though the menu was in French and nobody in the place spoke English. I mean, you would think that FRENCH FRIES would make for easy translation, but they call them Piveau Portes or something.

Just outside of Drummondville, we picked up two hitchhikers. Hitchhikers are much more common in Canada than they are here and generally seem to be normal enough people, as opposed to the freshly-paroled axe-murderers who thumb our nation's highways. It was raining and I felt that we should stop for the two punk-looking girls on the shoulder. Ignoring the protests of everyone else in the van, I pulled over and backed up for them.

They began thanking us (I presume) in French.

"We're Americans," I said. "We don't speak your language."

The beautiful blonde girl spoke up.

"I am Marie-Eve. Thanks for stopping."

"What's your name?" I asked the other one as I pulled back out onto the highway.

"She is France," answered Marie-Eve. "She speaks just French."

"Where ya goin'?"

"Quebec."

"Well that's where we're going too."

The girls conversed and giggled amongst themselves.

"How old are you?" I asked.

"Sixteen. France is fifteen."

God help me, Marie-Eve was the best looking sixteen-year-old girl I'd ever seen. Portia knew what I was thinking. She promptly smacked me on the head and hissed, "She's only sixteen, you dirty old pervert!"

I was determined to make conversation, even though the one who spoke English spoke it poorly. They claimed to be going to Quebec to visit some friends. I asked them if they were familiar with the Riverdales. They weren't. They did, however, know our other band, Screeching Weasel. I couldn't tell whether or not they were impressed. Marie-Eve pulled out a big, fat joint.

"Do you have a lighter?" she asked.

"Don't smoke that thing in here," I said. "We're punks, not hippies. And if we get pulled over, you're gonna eat that thing."

She didn't understand.

"Eat it, y'know, if the policio stop us, manga the fuckin' pot." I wasn't sure what language I was speaking but they got the message.

Marv the Roadie, who was riding shotgun, suggested that there was something more to their story than just hitchhiking to Quebec to meet friends. I decided to find out what their game was. I started out slowly.

"Don't you worry about somebody raping you or killing you?" I asked. "Hitchhiking can be dangerous you know."

Marie-Eve reached in her purse and showed us a gigantic bullet.

"I have this."

"Well," I said, "if you don't have a gun to shoot it, it ain't gonna do you much good."

She pulled out a little knife about the size of a file on a nail clipper.

"I have this, too."

"Whattya gonna do with that?"

"Stab."

I dropped the lecture and started needling them until they gave me the goods. The real story came out a little at a time. They were in what they called a "bad girls school." They'd gotten permission to go to a punk rock show in Drummondville that night but had decided instead to go see some friends in Quebec.

"So you're fugitives?"

Marie-Eve looked at me questioningly.

"You're two bad girls," I said.

She nodded happily.

"This is great," I said. "We've got two underage girls on unauthorized leave from a reform school or a rehab center carrying a bullet, a pee-wee knife and a couple of grams of pot. If we get pulled over I'm just gonna shoot myself and get it over with."

"You're the one who wanted to pick them up," said Marv.

"Shut up," I answered, turning my attention back to our delinquents. God only knew what kind of fucked-up French-Canadian laws we had already broken just by picking these two rascals up.

"You're going to see your boyfriends?"

"No," she said, giggling. "Just friends."

"Well, why don't you call them and bring them to the show? You can get backstage. It'll be fun."

"No, we can't. We have to see our friends. We promised."

"What friends? They don't like punk rock? Hey, they might not have heard of the Riverdales but everybody knows Green Day."

"Oh, we like Green Day and we like Screeching Weasel but we have to see our friends. We have to pick something up."

"What?"

They spoke gibberish to each other for a while. Finally, the beautiful, sixteen-year-old Marie-Eve spoke.

"PCP."

"Angel Dust?!?" I was shocked. "What are you, fucking nuts?" I'd heard that shit was popular among the French-Canadian punks but I'd never really believed it. Having had some experience with said drug in my youth, I started my lecture. I stopped in mid-sentence. I realized I was old. I didn't have a fucking clue. I was about as cool as their parents.

"Well," I said. "You should really stick to pot and beer. That shit's bad news."

"We don't use it," she said. "We buy, then we bring it back and sell at the show. Then we make money and leave the bad girls school and get our apartment."

"Good plan," I offered. "So now," I said to no one in particular, "We've got the 'two bad girls' — ages fifteen and sixteen — on unauthorized leave from a reform school or a rehab center carrying a bullet, a peewee knife and a couple of grams of pot and we're taking them to Quebec to buy angel dust so they can sell it to other sixteen-year-old girls."

"You're the one who wanted to pick them up," said Marv.

I ignored the urge to slit his throat with the nail clippers and instead started praying that the gendarmes wouldn't allow my virgin ass to be violated by some greasy, hairy crack-smoker named Pierre.

We finally arrived at the Colisee de Quebec and got out of the van. The girls agreed to pose for a picture with us. As we stood for the photo, I asked them how they'd vote in the referendum if they were old enough. Marie-Eve translated for France.

"*Oui, oui,*" they both answered.

"That's good," I said. "Very good."

We said goodbye and wished them luck with their drug deal.

After the show, we headed out to the van. Marv picked up a little black change purse with a note on top that had been left under our windshield wiper. It read:

"Look in the black bag. we write us a message."

I brought the bag into the van and opened it. Inside was the following note:

"see you guys! take care of you! tank's for the lift. Ive wish you to have a lot of fun to do your show. We love you all. We are in very big fuck because we cannot see your show.

Bye
Marie-Eve XXX
France XXX
the too bad girl."

After the gig in Ottawa the next night, we left for Halifax. Driving through Quebec, somebody mentioned that if the referendum went through today, we could be shut off from the rest of the world.

"They will not," I said emphatically, "under any circumstances, vote *oui*. And even if they do, the Quebec government will screw around with the numbers so it comes out close, but no *oui*."

We reached Halifax in mid-afternoon. I needed new underwear. I was in a goofy mood, as I often am after an all-night trip. I rode shotgun while Marv drove. It had been raining earlier so the streets were slick.

"I need underwear, underwear, underwear," I chanted.

We were coming up to a stoplight when I saw a department store to my right.

"Yo Marv!" I yelled. "I can get some underwear right there!"

I turned back just in time to watch as the little car in front of us stopped at the yellow light and Marv hit the brakes. We slid into the car, somehow with enough time for me to advise everybody to hold on. Marv backed up a bit from the car. The rear end was completely caved in. We got out and checked the Econoline. There was a tiny dent above the bumper. The guy driving the car stepped out and approached us.

"I'm really sorry," said Marv.

"Oh, it could've happened to anybody, eh?"

A cop showed up and filled out a report. He informed us that our plates had expired.

"I hate to do this, but you'll have to come with me and pay a fine," he said. He really did look sorry about the whole thing, like he'd rather invite us out for a donut and a cold beer.

We paid the ticket. Portia and I spent the rest of the day in bed watching the news, which was saturated with reports on the vote. Finally it was all over but the shouting. The separatists had lost by a narrow margin. I opened a beer and watched the Bears game until I couldn't keep my eyes open any longer.

For at least another decade, all was again peaceful in Canada. I slept like a baby.

THE NEW PUNK ORDER

Most of the things that are wrong with punk are pretty much the same things that have always been wrong with punk. It's just a matter of percentages. For example, ten years ago there were far fewer bands in existence in underground music than now, and out of those bands there were really only a handful that had any relevance to punk. And out of *those*, maybe ten percent were good.

In 1998, there are so many bands that could be considered relevant to punk that it's impossible for anyone to keep up with them all. Naturally, only about one percent of them are any good. But because of the large number of them, there are still more good bands around now than there were in 1988. (And so it follows that there are so many more bad ones too, and they're so bad it's like a punch in the nose. Or, perhaps more appropriately, a kick in the ass.)

But with the punk rock explosion of the mid-nineties some things really *did* change. Instead of there being a few well-concealed doors leading to a winding path that ended up at an underground cavern, the entire lid was blown off the punk rock encampment and anybody who happened to wander by was able to stroll in and make themselves at home.

At first, I tried not to be a prick about it (hell, my income doubled in 1995 — I wasn't about to start tossing out blanket condemnations) (if it makes you feel any better, my income is back to slightly above meager now that punk is no longer the flavor of the moment) (in short, if I don't pump out a new record every year, I get to go back to tallying up gas and Ho-Ho purchases at the Shell mini-mart). None of us were born with mohawks, I asserted. We should afford these people the same courtesies that we were shown back when we didn't know much of anything outside of the soporific realm of mainstream pop culture. We shouldn't be scaring them away, I said. We should let 'em look around, see if some bells start ringing. After all, most of us in punk were some form of fucked-up loser rejected from society. We'd been excluded from every clique and social club. We didn't fit in anywhere and we knew it. The closest we came to fitting in somewhere was at a punk rock show, and even then we were constantly arguing with each other. We were desperate for our own clique but at the same time we were apparently genetically mandated to follow a course of unwavering individuality; we had to say something when something needed to be said — and even when it didn't; we had to provide a contrary opinion, often just for the sake of doing it.

Of course, not everybody in punk ten years ago was a quirky, engaging individual. Most people weren't. But the people who grabbed a microphone or a typewriter and started mouthing off in 1988 were infinitely more fascinating than the toads who are running the show in 1998. The majority of the movers and shakers in punk were *characters* — people with strong, often *weird*, personalities; people who were usually intelligent and witty (despite often trying to play down those qualities); people who constantly questioned and weren't afraid to confront stupidity. No, most of the people in punk rock were not like an enthralling combination of Cary Grant, H.L. Mencken and Liberace. But the people who *were* engaging, articulate, insane, funny and/or outrageous were the people who made things happen; the fanzine publishers, band members, promoters. They set the tone and ran the show. Those people can come from anywhere, and when punk rock became momentarily glamorous in 1994 and 1995 I didn't think it was my place to be running off those newcomers who could potentially make punk more exciting, intelligent, funny or bizarre.

In retrospect, maybe I should've used the little rats for target practice.

What's wrong with punk in 1998 is that the people who are setting the tone — the people in bands, the fanzine publishers and show promoters — are the same type of weak-willed, mealy-mouthed, dull purveyors of mediocrity that we used to laugh at. From whence came these yammering, witless trolls? Who knows, but I know who let them in.

It was our own fault, naturally — punks are nothing if not self-defeating. When the success of Green Day and The Offspring blew the top off of an exclusive club (one, by the way, that had become increasingly provincial; something *needed* to blow) and the mainstream kids started filing in and putting their feet up on our coffee table, nobody was there to set examples. We were too slow to realize that the time had come to provide some subtle guidance; there were just too many new people around at the same time to hope that they'd all be able to clue in if left to their own devices. If we weren't careful, they'd bring in their own reality — the one of mainstream pop culture — and we'd be left on the outside. We weren't careful. Hence the waterheads.

MaximumRockNRoll — the one magazine that probably could've made a difference — became even more pedantic than it had always been, laying down more and more rules, forcing people to make decisions that shouldn't have been forced on them. It had negative results and why wouldn't it? Punks don't like being told they have to adhere to rules. Your rules are bullshit, people started to reason, so that probably means that pretty much *everything* you say is bullshit.

Older punks, myself included, weren't prepared to deal with an influx of youth that had somehow come to adolescence in the nineties without understanding things that we all took for granted; that bands like Nirvana were lame; that MTV was for chumps; that racism, homophobia and sexism are just hoops designed to keep class divisions intact (and that knee-jerk, anti-racist liberalism that refuses to acknowledge the more repulsive cultural traits found in all groups [even — gasp! — non-white, non-male and non-heterosexual groups] is just another hoop); that our economic system is based on maintaining the worst aspects of society. Instead of rising to the challenge, we retreated, bitter and jaded, into self-involvement.

Many of the older punks finally turned into regular adults and started spending their nights in bars drinking and bopping to the sounds of a hundred sound-alike rock and roll bands. They sneered at any band that was more than marginally popular and they got agitated over any band that dared to write lyrics with any social relevance. They didn't need to be reminded about racism and sexism, they claimed. They already *knew* all that. Meanwhile, they developed angry white man attitudes on social issues and became cynical and ultimately *boring* rock and roll versions of thirty-something disco dancers and ravesters. They somehow managed to turn apoliticism into an extreme act. They became as pigheaded and pedantic as the political punks at whom they still sneered. Viewing themselves as hipper and wiser than their younger counterparts in the subculture, they still somehow managed to cling even more desperately to a naive and opaque worldview: popular bands were no good; too many records were too slickly produced; anything that didn't sink the mercury on their hip-ometer was pap for mall-rats (all of which might explain why this music — the raw rock and roll of bands like the New Bomb Turks and Teengenerate — was championed by MRR despite the overtly leftist agenda of the magazine, which for years had resulted in correct lyrical sentiments being placed far above musical greatness in evaluating the quality of a band. The attitudes that seemed to go hand in hand with the punk 'n' roll style of music had the same fundamentalist tone — though considerably more snide — that had once been behind MRR's allegiance to hundreds of terrible, generic hardcore bands).

Unfortunately, the hipster douchebags were mostly right; too much music *was* radio friendly; calculated, lacking spontaneity. But I felt the same way about bands like the Humpers. I saw it as contrived fluff designed to lull drunken thirty-something losers with demeaning white collar cubicle jobs into a fantasy land where for a few hours a week they didn't feel like washed-up jerks who had given up. I didn't like the music made by aging slacker never-weres any more than I liked the aspiring yuppie snobs who listened to it. But the alternative wasn't any better.

Bands started spending ludicrous sums of money to make albums. Naturally, their records were overproduced, often sounding eerily similar to the alternative rock being pumped out of FM stations and MTV faster than you could say Tommy Hilfiger. They were professional punks who used studio effects and precision musicianship (the bands weren't just "tight," they were mathematical) to try to make up for their lack of songwriting ability and conviction. They'd obviously taken lessons to learn how to play their instruments.

This stuff — much of which was either horrible NOFX and Bad Religion rip-offs or even more horrible Green Day, Screeching Weasel and Queers rip-offs — simply had no heart. Punk rock bands were supposed to have something — anything — to say and a need to say it. These bands came off as calculating musicians who were in a band as a career choice, not out of any need to stand up and say — or scream — something, whether it be a political manifesto or "Fuck you, asshole!" They didn't seem to feel the need to make music as an antidote to the crap on the radio; they seemed happier *copying* the crap on the radio. From the generic hardcore sounds of the California bands that seemed to exist solely to perform for backwards ball cap-wearing, bong-toting, goatee-sporting Gen X snowboarders and perpetually enraged, drunken, bare-chested muscleheads at Pepsi-sponsored festivals to the bland, by-the-numbers sounds of a slew of mediocre pop-punk bands (most of whom went heavy on the pop and real, real light on the punk — if they didn't forget it altogether), these bands had career move written all over them.

The snowboard bands were at least occasionally offensive, much like the heavy metal heroes from whom they swiped their sound. But the pop-punkers were the Pat Boones of punk rock — taking relevant, exciting music and sucking the life out of it to make it presentable to boring, vacant-eyed, clean-cut kids; creating Wonder Bread tunes that seldom raised the ire of concerned parents and other wary authority figures. It was the kind of stuff you could dance with your sister to. If singing hopelessly corny songs about wanting to take a cute girl to the movies wasn't bad enough, things got to the point where wussy lollipop punk bands were preaching fundamentalist Christianity. Nobody questioned it.

In fact, nobody questioned anything. So many things that we had taken for granted for years had suddenly become verboten in the New Punk Order.

Fucking was out; cuddling and holding hands was in.

Cranky fanzine editors pushing their own agendas were a thing of the past; a thousand newsprint monstrosities took their place; passionless wastes of pulp staffed by geeks looking to move up the corporate ladder. They seldom gave negative reviews to records and never to records released by their advertisers; they were essentially trade magazines. Some of these fanzine editors didn't even know the difference between an album and an EP (how could you possibly get to the point of writing, editing and publishing a fanzine without knowing what an EP is???).

Singers who walked on stage and entranced you with their charisma, eccentricities, obnoxiousness or just plain insanity disappeared; different was bad and the demonization of anything resembling mental unbalance ensured that the character was sucked out of music. Pop-punk bands started staring at their shoes and thanking their politely applauding audiences with all the genuine humility of Jerry Lewis scooting his ass along the floor while gagging on a mouthful of marbles. The snowboard bands put on their frat party-style shows with the crowd-working savvy of a Wayne Newton while their thick-skulled followers brought sales of dorky oversized t-shirts, sweatshirts and ball caps to a new high, accused each other of faggotry while standing shirtless together in the pit — much too close for any objective outsider to see their activities as heterosexual — and pummeled one another like the lumbering apes from whom they appeared to have only recently evolved.

And worst of all, biting, sometimes necessarily brutal commentary was a thing of the past. "It's all good," the multi-headed crowd monster shouted. Everyone has a right to their opinion, and the right to not be criticized for it. I'm not into that band but it's cool if you are; I won't knock them because, gee, they're worth something to you ("I'm okay, you're okay!"). Don't criticize anything or anyone but the most obvious targets; to do so is to risk generating the nastiest insult the New Punk Order can hurl: You're closed-minded. Oh, the horror!

Vanilla. Mainstream. Normal. Everything's okay. And if you disagree, your only alternative is sitting over a glass of overpriced beer in some shitty dive with a bunch of other losers listening to the thrilling sounds of yet another band of hipsters covering "I'm Stranded" by the Saints. Or if you're too young to get into those clubs, you can romanticize boring unknown bands, inflating their one or two minor positive qualities only because it's such a joy to finally like a band whose t-shirts aren't worn by the people at your school who beat you up. Problem is, most of those bands are usually unknown for very good reasons.

And above all, if you're into pop punk, you better know that a band isn't judged anymore on whether they're good or bad. What we're concerned with now is, "Are they nice?"

Did the bass player talk to you after the show? Did they answer your letters, give you free merch and sign autographs for you? Yes? Okay, that means they're a good band, because the New Punk Order is a little like Catholicism — intentions are what counts. They seem to be doing it for the right reasons, so they must be good. They're good people, so they must be in a good band. What used to be the polite way of saying a band sucked — "They're really nice people" — has become the benchmark by which the quality of a band is judged. The New Punk Order wants to be lied to — desperately. Tell us you're not in it for the money. Smile at us, appreciate and respect us, *love* us.

We are the New Punk Order and we don't know any better. We came from the mainstream. This is how it's always been done in our world. You're supposed to make us believe that you feel the same way we do; that we're all in this together; that if there weren't so many people here I could meet you and shake your hand and be your friend. Sure, deep down we suspect it might not be true but we want the goddamn illusion, okay? So smile and shake my fucking hand, asshole, and try not to spend it all in one place.

I must stop typing now. You never know when the New Punk Order might be listening, and I don't want to spend the night suffering the abuses of the Pop-Punk Goon Squad, strapped to my high-backed ergonomically correct office chair with Scotch Tape (the dumb fuckers don't even carry duct tape); eyelids prodded open *Clockwork Orange*-style as I'm forced to read the last 10 months of alt.punk messages on the Internet, while the headphones that they've Krazy-glued to my head assault my defenseless ears with an endless, horrific loop of the Voodoo Glowskulls, The Promise Ring and MxPx; and as a final, cruel insult, the backpack-toting bunnypunks replace my nude Traci Lords poster with a triple-sized blow-up of the cover of the latest issue of *Punk Planet*.

Of course I'm just kidding. We all know the New Punk Order doesn't run around using force to shut up the opinionated, contrary people in punk rock. After all, they don't need to. Everybody's more than happy to shut up voluntarily.

CLOWN FOR HIRE

Author's note: "Clown For Hire" and "Good Doggy" were written for Hit List, *a magazine that was started up after Tim Yohannan's death. Its publisher, Jeff Bale, was a co-founder of* MaximumRockNRoll. *What Jeff wanted out of me was the pit bull image I'd cultivated for five and a half years in my columns in MRR. The problem was, I was tired of being a clown, as is reflected in the second half of the column. My second column for* Hit List *was rejected; it was the first chapter of my then unpublished novel,* Like Hell, *which was eventually published by Hope And Nonthings. Jeff had told me that I could write whatever I wanted but by the second issue he'd changed his mind. I realized that Jeff only wanted goon material from me so I submitted the column that I've titled "Good Doggy," hoping that he'd understand the point I was making: sure I can do this crap, and it's mildly entertaining for a few seconds, but it has no substance. Jeff didn't get my point. He thought the column was terrific. I quit soon after.*

It's probably a sign of my slowly improving mental health that I haven't had a whole lot to say on the subject of punk rock for the past few years. Sure, I was canned from *MaximumRockNRoll*; Tim didn't want me subverting the troops or something. I took it as a compliment. I didn't have anything left to say anyway. When Bale got canned, we all knew it wasn't because he was writing things in his column with which Tim disagreed; it was that Tim started seeing that people were taking the column *seriously*.

Tim's dead now but I hear through the usual sources that his half-sane ghost is still making most of the editorial decisions over at MRR. The grapevine says that sometimes you can smell his spectral cigarette smoke in the hallways of MRR headquarters, which seems odd; Tim quit smoking a few years before he died. I've had no spooky nocturnal visits from the spirit of Tim Yo, but maybe that's just because I made him promise not to haunt me. He said I'd become too cynical and jaded, at least in regards to punk rock. It didn't seem worth it to search my soul to figure out if he was right.

So we're all supposed to pretend that this new rag isn't in competition with MRR. Right. Bale calls me up and asks me to write a column. I've gotten a total of one other offer since 1995 so I'm not about to turn it down; I have an ego to feed. But I'm immediately faced with a rule so silly that I have no choice but to break it in the second paragraph of my first column in the premiere issue. This magazine *is* in competition with MRR, and *Punk Planet* too, and it's gonna kick both their asses. Whether it is the publishers' intention or not really doesn't matter. And considering the competition, it won't take much to lead the pack. MRR is a trade magazine written by people who don't read, featuring record reviews by people who don't like music, all in the name of promoting a pseudo-anarchist manifesto that most of its readers ignore. *Punk Planet* is an inappropriately titled rag filled with nothing more than the latest developments in the world of bunny-punk as reported breathlessly by faux-jaded Gen-X cretins; its columnists are third-rate hacks whose idea of insight is whining about the lack of an affordable natural food store in the town where they're attending "university"; and its editor is a petty art fag who wouldn't know good writing if it crawled up his leg and gave him head.

That's rule number two. Don't get personal. What the fuck? Why call me?

After all, I'm an obedient little pup but I's only knows one trick, massuh... bark bark... take off my leash and yell, "sic"... I'll tear your fucking eyeballs out... stomp 'em into jelly with my white Converse Chuck Taylor All-Star hi-tops... I'll be the one in the leather jacket... talk about sick... unhealthy... low-brow comedy... I was a red-assed baboon... a zoo monkey too dumb to know that if you're gonna whack off in front of a crowd you should at least have the dignity not to do it with a huge grin plastered on your face... knock what you can't have... or don't understand... a clockwork orange... I really *didn't* understand... I still don't quite get it... I used to drink a lot when I wrote... chain smoke... three packs in eight hours... anybody who tells you that drugs don't help is either a Christian or a reformed addict... when I was at my happiest I never had anything to say... a few more milligrams of Klonopin a day... I had one month that was just fucking beautiful... 4:30 A.M. in a hotel room in Munich, a *swank* hotel... sitting on the edge of the bed with my Mosrite... writing pretty little songs like I was the only man in the world who knew how... I'm off drugs now... haven't been drunk in years... chewing on toothpicks that still remind me of cigarettes... funny thing though... can't write for shit... punching a lot of walls lately...

"What's it like to be a middle-aged punk?"... you're supposed to hang out in dingy bars... try to pick up other sad, lonely ex-punks... rock and roll rebel for the night... music courtesy of another bunch of too-cool rockers copying the Dolls or Iggy... painting by numbers... beer by the pitcher... cruising on fumes... drink up because tomorrow you go back to the cubicle... laugh to yourself at your co-workers who like Springsteen... you're still a small fish in a smaller pond... going gently into that good night... those of us who can't or won't aren't any better... just doomed to see the reality of our shitty lives a little more clearly... the months rush by so fast you start to realize you'll never win... and once you've seen the truth you can't ever make yourself forget... alcohol only works for so long... tell the lie to teenage kids?... now *that's* fucking cruel!... everything will *not* be okay... you laugh at yourself... not in some humorous, self-deprecating way... it's a mean laugh...

I don't even listen to rock and roll anymore... I swear to god... most of it sounds like noise to me... I hate kids... they've got too much energy and pointless enthusiasm... I want them to give up now... see your future like watching an old man whip open his raincoat to give you an eyeful of filthy crotch... "Youth is wasted on the young"... they'd rather hold hands than fuck... they believe in God... think they're going to go to hell if they're bad... they don't know that hell is for the stupid and weak and they already live in it... no idea how much they'll regret all the times they could've gotten fucked... fucked up... quit their jobs... don't get personal?... wrong number, pal... controversy?... I don't know the meaning of the word... I'm not playing dumb... don't ask me to try... I belch and halfway across the world some jerk gets a wild hair across his ass... I can't explain it... I'm a pussycat... I don't try anymore... can't try... takes too much out of me... not worth the effort.... it's not cynicism, it's intelligence... everything still sucks... it's just that now you're not lying to yourself about it... not exactly a tidal wave of an insight... I might not be able to learn new tricks... doesn't mean I have to keep repeating the old ones... should've called me for this gig back when I still gave half a fuck about being king of the shitpile... thanks for asking... but you know me... you know I'm probably gonna hate this rag so much that in six months I'll be knocking it in some other rag...

GOOD DOGGY

Stupid questions and comments I'm sick of hearing, or... Shut your fucking traps you little pissants.

Your band was so much better back in 19__. Your vocals suck now and so do your lyrics.
My band sucked back in 19__. We played derivative, contrived nonsense with an occasional decent tune thrown in. I'm ten times the singer and lyricist I was back in 19__ and if you had any taste or brains you'd know that.

The band was so much better when (insert any one of fifteen ex-band member names) were in it. The new guys suck. It's just not the same band.
Of course it's not the same band. That's the whole point. It's better. (Insert any one of fifteen ex-band member names) were pains in the asses who showed up to band practice hung over and looking like they'd rather be anywhere else. They got paid a disproportionate amount of money for working all of two months a year but they were still always too goddamn busy to rehearse the songs that put food on their table. Their apathy and lack of interest in anything other than collecting their royalty checks and posing for photographs made the band suck for me and ever since I lanced those boils it's been nothing but sunshine and lollipops around here. If you like

those stooges so much, why don't you go listen to *their* fucking bands? And by the way, the new guys don't suck; they are superb. You suck.

When is your band coming to my town? Why don't you tour?
We're not *ever* coming to your town because your town is a depressing, worthless piece of shit that only exists so loser nobodies like yourself don't take up valuable space in real cities. We don't tour because we hate you. Think about it, if *you* had to be around you for more than five minutes, wouldn't you be gnawing your own leg off to get out of the trap? If my band ever plays shows again, we'll play them in the only three cities that matter in this country: Chicago, New York and Philadelphia. And Philly's only on the list because you can do a matinee in the afternoon and go watch Sabu take the sickest of bumps at the ECW Arena in the evening.

If you hate music so much why do you play it?
I don't hate music. I hate *bad* music; like almost everything that ever gets released. I play music because I feel it's my civic duty to do well what so many others do poorly.

I hate pop punk. Your band and those other Lookout bands are responsible for all that shitty pop punk out there.
Pipe down, moron. I had nothing to do with all those crappy pop-punk bands. It's not *my* goddamn fault that so many talentless, idiotic fuckheads decided my band was a good starting point for their own embarrassing careers in music. Why the hell are you even listening to all those terrible bands anyway?

Why do you like sports so much? Competition sucks.
Only losers don't like competition. Maybe you don't like sports because you're a pussy or a weakling. Just because you totally suck at something doesn't mean you can't enjoy watching others do it well. I don't *play* sports because I'm not good at them. But I don't *hate* sports because I suck at them. And I don't go ahead and try to play sports anyway just because I *like* them. Then I would be like all you idiots who play in god awful punk bands just because you like music and regardless of the fact that your bands totally blow. Like Dirty Harry said, "A man's gotta know his limitations." But then again, most of you aren't men. You're boys.

Okay, but how can you like wrestling? It's fake.
So is punk rock and you like *that*, dumb ass.

I'm a Christian and I'd like to ask...
Shut the fuck up.

Your writing used to be so much better back when you wrote for *MaximumRockNRoll*. What the fuck?
I've gotten a whole lot more intelligent. Now everything I say floats miles above your pointed little heads. It's not that I'm a worse writer; it's that I'm a lot smarter and you're a lot dumber.

Over and out.

CRIMPSHRINE

For my money, the most important of the first four Lookout releases was Crimpshrine's "Sleep, What's That?" EP. Over the years, Operation Ivy has been singled out as the band that was the backbone of Lookout and the East Bay scene of the late 1980s, and it's hard to argue otherwise. OPIV was a tremendous band and one of the most crucial ones in setting the tone for what punk rock bands would sound like in the '90s. But Crimpshrine was the heart and soul of the East Bay, and the best band to come out of the Gilman/Lookout scene.

I first heard the songs from "Sleep, What's That?" on a tape given to me by a friend in early 1988. The tape also included "Re-Arranged," the song that appeared on *MaximumRockNRoll*'s "Turn It Around" compilation. I'd already dubbed an Operation Ivy demo from a friend and gotten an advance copy of the songs that would be released on Iscoracy's "Bedtime For Isocracy" EP and they were brilliant, but Crimpshrine seemed to embody the best aspects of those bands while adding a melancholy twist, and a visceral, palpable passion. I was simply blown away when I heard the Crimpshrine songs. Not since I'd first heard the Ramones had a band had such an immediate impact on me. Within days I was writing my own songs that were heavily influenced by Crimpshrine. I listened to the tape over and over, trying to take it all in.

The band was sloppy and they hadn't been recorded particularly well, and yet it was obvious that guitarist/singer Jeff Ott and bassist Pete

Rypins were at least as talented musically as the mullet-haired heshers who roamed the streets of suburbia with their Jackson guitars and thousand-dollar demo tapes featuring self-indulgent attempts to showcase their musicianship. But much more importantly, the band wrote deceptively simple-sounding songs, and those songs were brilliant.

Crimpshrine combined the basic feel of punk legends like Stiff Little Fingers and the Buzzcocks with an almost hippie-esque, Jimi Hendrix influence that relied heavily on heart-wrenching melody and a desperate feel to the playing. Lyrically, they combined personal politics and issues of social change effortlessly and with a conviction not seen since the days of the Dead Kennedys and MDC. They had all the aggression and power of those bands, but they also had beautiful, angst-ridden melodies and a lyrical genuineness (and maybe naiveté) of the sort that was frowned on in independent music circles in 1988. But if their politics were a product of their influences from the past, the execution was purely original and firmly rooted in the present. Jeff Ott sang the words written by himself and drummer Aaron Cometbus as if his life and yours depended on it; you couldn't help but be both impressed and worried that Jeff might be screaming his vocal chords into a permanent, bloody mess. But Jeff wasn't simply a screamer; his voice was a barely-controlled, urgent plea that hit you in the heart like a bullet.

I was thrilled when, upon my first visit to the Bay Area, Jeff and Aaron took my band down to Telegraph Avenue and showed us their Berkeley, which included trying to break into locked rooms at the University of California and flying paper airplanes off of the top of one of the university's buildings. The idea was, of course, spearheaded by Jeff, who always had a sly, knowing, almost insane look in his eye that convinced you within seconds of meeting him that he was on the verge of changing the world. Jeff had a lot of ideas — plenty of them crazy — but few of them that went long without being put into action.

After listening to me make fun of the East Bay habit of using the slang term "hella" as an all-purpose adverb, Aaron gently took me by the wrist and wrote "HELLUV" in large letters on my hand with a Sharpie, to remind me of the proper pronunciation of his beloved malapropism. When I arrived back home in suburban Chicago, I was a different person, and Crimpshrine was a big part of the reason why.

Later that summer, when Crimpshrine's aborted tour left Jeff and Aaron stranded in Florida without a drummer, I drove down with a friend and picked them up. They stayed with Jughead and me for three weeks. While awaiting the arrival of Paul, their new bassist, they taught us

Crimpshrine songs on the bass so we could fill in and they could play the few gigs they had set up in the Midwest. They would break up within a year.

Crimpshrine went on to record another EP, "Quit Talkin' Claude," with Paul on bass this time. The album (which had been recorded prior to the departure of Pete and second guitarist Idon) that then-Lookout president Lawrence Livermore rejected would turn up in parts on various compilations and another album. Thankfully, Lookout has released that material along with other barely-heard tracks on *Duct Tape Soup* and *The Sound Of A New World Being Born*.

After the band broke up, Aaron went back to writing and publishing *Cometbus*, the fanzine he'd been doing since he was thirteen and which he still publishes today. He continues to play in part-time bands such as Pinhead Gunpowder. He recently published his first novel, *Double Duce*, a world-weary and hilarious story of life in a punk house. Jeff formed Fifteen, a logical, if more political, extension of Crimpshrine. Both of them continue to contribute to the punk scene with a purpose and conviction seldom seen in people over the age of eighteen.

PRACTICE DOES NOT MAKE PERFECT

I've been running on and off since I was ten years old. My father — an ex-Marine — bought me a pair of good running shoes (Brooks — the only brand I'll ever wear for running) and I used to run with him during the brief period when he'd given up his Camel non-filters. I joined the track and field team in junior high school but I despised the competition and though I was very fast, I had no motivation to win and thus, was always a middle-of-the-pack boy. I don't know if my father's competitive spirit hadn't been transferred to me genetically or if my hatred of him had caused me to reject the things he most fondly embraced, but I was a dishrag when it came to sports.

My father had been on the wrestling team in high school. Naturally I wrestled. But I was a lazy wrestler and would give in to pain easily, much more easily than I had to. He may have thought his son was gay; but even at the vulnerable time when I was entering puberty and was worried about all the things boys on the verge of adolescence worry about, I got a vague sense of satisfaction out of the thought of the old man fretting over the possibility that he'd sired a queer.

My father had been a catcher on his high school baseball team and for three years — from the time I was seven until I was ten — he coached my Little League team, which meant that I was the team's catcher. There was little point in arguing with him over taking on this unsavory role on the team. I took my spot behind home plate, hating every minute of it. Getting knocked in the head by wayward bats; getting steamrolled by desperate youths rounding third, fiercely intent on scoring; chasing after hopeless foul balls, my shin guards slamming against my knees; removing my gear for my inevitable strike out, ground out or, if I was lucky, fly out; going through the seemingly endless process of putting my gear back on to take the field and more abuse; I went limp. For many years I felt this was a character flaw. It was only as an adult that I realized that I wasn't weak; I subconsciously tanked at any time during which my father was praying to whatever gods he believed in that I'd be strong. I moved slowly on the field and goofed off during the team's excruciatingly long practice sessions and I got yelled at back home for my attitude, but seeing him pissed off — and let down — was almost worth the misery of being subjected to his diatribes and occasional beatings with "The Belt."

The one year when I'd moved up to the middle league at age eleven and played ball when my father wasn't my coach, I'd played surprisingly well, switching off between second base and left field. Without my father's interference, I made the all-star team that year as a starter, along with Bobby Murcer's son, who was technically too young to be in the league and was an alternate. I knocked in several home runs that season playing for the Prospect Heights League Yankees, but I was primarily a reasonably sound fielder with a strong if not particularly accurate arm and a speed which gained me many doubles and triples which should have rightfully been singles, or in many cases, easy throw-outs. I was daring and would invariably try for the extra base, aware of the multitude of faltering throws, catches and tags of my opponents. I had fun in my last year of baseball and my entire team — most of whom would end up as juvenile delinquents just like me — reveled in beating our opponents on the field when we couldn't beat them on the scoreboard: our pitchers threw bean balls over the slightest perturbance and our runners — myself primary among them — slid into bases cleats high — going for the fielders' balls — when trying to beat out a throw. It was not my father's brand of baseball; in fact it was thuggery, and I loved it.

Like many sons, I couldn't wait for the day when I'd be big enough and strong enough to beat my drunken, idiot, asshole father to a bloody pulp; like many sons, when that day came, I'd gained the maturity to restrain myself and I'd gained the insight into human character to realize that for better or worse my father was simply a man and in spite of his shortcomings, he had only wanted the best for me. When I had experienced firsthand the difficulties of working shitty, demeaning jobs in order to put food on the table just for MYSELF, I learned to respect my father for doing the same for an entire family even though most men — including myself — would have taken off at the first opportunity.

I gave up running when I discovered marijuana and liquor and speed and opium and other fun drugs but I took it back up in 1990 when my metabolism changed and my beer gut started making me conspicuous in public, and when I'd forgiven my father for his sins, both real and imagined. Since then, I've been an on again/off again runner but unlike in my youth, I now run for the pure joy of it. I realize that running temporarily causes weight loss and I'm aware that common knowledge dictates that aerobic exercise is good for humans — especially people with faulty hearts like mine — but I'm also aware of the seemingly irrefutable studies which claim that running doesn't actually do one much good in terms of an overall exercise program and that, in fact, because of the many injuries associated with running, it may actually be more dangerous to one's health than laying on the couch watching sitcoms. None of this really matters to me because as I stated, I run for the joy of it. And when I say I run, I should point out that technically I jog; I simply prefer the word "run." Nothing of much interest happens on my runs; I just move, breathe and sweat.

I always have a tune in my head when I run. It's usually the theme music from The Weather Channel, from which I always get the local forecast before I leave. Depending on the length of my run (anywhere from two to five miles depending on my schedule and the weather), this can get monotonous, but only once I realize it's in my head. When I catch it, I'll consciously change the tune. Just yesterday, in the middle of a brisk four-mile run, I had two discordant notes going in my head in time with my feet to the point where it became maddening; two insistent, nigh-demonic notes repeating incessantly like some deranged, skipping record of circus music. I actually ended up — for only the second time — having a panic attack while running, which really shouldn't be an altogether unusual experience as my heart rate is ALREADY up; I'm ALREADY sweating; I'm ALREADY experiencing many of the physical symptoms of a panic attack (which is probably why so many people who have panic attacks fear exercise). It was fairly hellish but I stuck it out and finished my run in spite of my distress.

As with meditation, running takes self-control, commitment and practice. I don't meditate; I practice meditation. Neither do I run; I practice running. Several well-meaning friends have suggested that I enter a race. But that would involve training. It would involve setting a goal — not necessarily to win, not necessarily even to compete, perhaps just to finish. But I believe it would ruin running for me. I run alone — running with a partner is a thought that appalls me — with no real goals and no real purpose. But that's not to say that the experience is entirely aimless; as I already stated, it's practice. Practice for the sake of practice and nothing more.

When I do something — a job, a project, anything goal-oriented, hobby-like in nature or necessary for keeping a roof over my head and food in my belly, I simply do it. There is a need and I fill it. It's simple and it has a point, but I rarely get anything out of it other than my primary goal, and sometimes a little aggravation (and sometimes a lot). I often lose interest. It becomes monotonous; a chore; a burden. I grow to resent it. What was once enjoyable, benign, or, at worst, mildly irritating begins to slowly suck the joy out of my soul. I become consumed with a dull, throbbing hostility. I will burn any bridge in order to escape the sour taste of familiarity with that which I've mastered and thus has become boring. This is why I've held few jobs for more than three consecutive months. It's why I tired of playing punk rock shows. It's why I constantly move ahead to other projects, other things to keep me interested, at least for a short while. Monotony is my enemy. Its only place is in my daily life, in taking care of my cats and myself. I feed the cats, clean their litter box, take them to the vet when they're sick, and I don't mind. I don't resent the dishes I have to wash, the water I drink, the food I eat; I don't resent my bowel movements or the emptying of my bladder; nor do I resent showers, shaving or cutting my fingernails. These are essential and they only bother me when I'm consumed with creative work. If there were any way to avoid these things, I would, but instead of hoping for miracles I've chosen to accept reality.

But when I practice, my experience always changes, usually in small and unintended ways. I gain a little insight, but only occasionally. The key is to just do it without JUST doing it; nothing more or less than practice simply for the sake of practicing. Having no expectations has, in my experience, led to insight, but it's never quite what I would've imagined.

I always stretch a little bit before I run and a little more afterwards. In the summer, I'll bring a small bottle of Gatorade with me to avoid dehydration, but I don't like to; I don't like to have to hold on to anything while I run. I wear my watch (a cheap Timex) and a wristband containing my house keys. If I'm on a long run, I'll do a slow first mile — about eleven minutes — then I'll work up to a nine or ten-minute mile (on a good day, eight) — which is still a bit slow, but probably a proper pace for a three-pack-a-day smoker. I'm sure when I quit (Next week? Next month?) I'll speed up. I occasionally sprint for the last quarter or half mile, but doing so in the summer is unwise; I often end up feeling like I'm going to barf or pass out or both.

Discourteous drivers always hear it from me. Those who don't understand the concept of a pedestrian's right of way; who barely brake at the stop sign before taking off again to beat me across the street. I'll usually yell "Motherfucker" or "Asshole" or some other crude, spontaneous word or phrase. They seldom slow down or stop when they hear it, but if they do, I invariably run straight at them; high on my own endorphins, the concept of potential physical harm never crosses my mind. So far, all of those I've sprinted towards have put their cars into drive and taken off.

I've had physical contact with a car only twice, and both times it was at my own initiation. The first time, I was running across a street on which I had the right of way; the perpendicular street had stop signs and mine didn't. A determined, middle-aged woman driving a green Mercedes-Benz had been waiting impatiently at her stop sign for eight seconds or so to cross the street over two lanes, hampered by the stream of traffic in both directions. Seeing a small opening, she decided to slam on the gas pedal to shoot past an oncoming bus; presumably she thought she'd pass me after she just barely got past the bus. She did, but only because I always keep my head up while running and only because I slowed down just in time; I've lived long enough to know that Mercedes-Benzes are usually driven by fools. The back of her car missed me by less than a foot but I had my wits enough about me to smack the trunk of the car with the side of my right fist, HARD. I yelled, "YOU CRAZY MOTHERFUCKING BITCH!" and kept running. She took off, perhaps still convinced that she'd clipped me and terrified of paying the price in a lawsuit. Maybe she slept uneasily for a night or two. I sincerely hope so.

The other time was when I was running in the rain this past summer. It was a fairly heavy downpour — around noon — and I'd been very careful around the stop signs as many drivers were skidding past the white line. I was on the right side of the street on the sidewalk when I came to a stop sign — a two-way stop sign. Traffic was moving freely on the street in front of me in either direction and I was planning on turning left to continue my jog. A line of several cars led by a silver Lexus was backed up at the stop sign. The Lexus driver was looking eagerly to his left to check for a break in the traffic in order to make his right turn. He didn't bother looking to his right to see the wet, sweaty, determined jogger about to cross his path. He made the turn without even glancing in my direction. I managed to avoid getting hit, but just barely. As I did with the Mercedes woman, I slammed the trunk of his car with my fist, but this time I got a particularly forceful, loud hit in. Pleased, if still slightly peeved, I continued on my run. Half a block later I heard "HEY FUCKHEAD!" I looked behind me and saw that the driver of the Lexus had turned around to confront me. Without thinking, I screamed "MOTHERFUCKER!" and ran across the stream of traffic towards his car. I stopped in front of the Lexus and yelled "DON'T YOU LOOK BOTH WAYS BEFORE YOU TURN YA STUPID FUCKIN' ASSHOLE??!"

"Fuck you!" he screeched, this prissy yuppie twerp in his shirt and tie. "RIGHT OF WAY!" I yelled, following my declaration with bellowed obscenities and a rhythmic pounding on the hood of his car with my fists, occasionally stopping my ranting long enough to dare him to get out of his car and call me a fuckhead while out of the safety of his vehicle. There was a line of traffic behind him that was backed up for a block. I imagine that I was quite a sight; I'd pulled the hood of my sweatshirt down to reveal a shaven, gleaming, dripping skull and was indicating through words and actions that I was daring — no, BEGGING — him to get out of his car and face me. Finally, I controlled myself enough to kick his grill with a Brooks-clad foot and then turned and ran back across the street. He turned back around at the next street but I was unsettled and finished my run early, unsatisfied and furious at this yuppie for ruining my otherwise peaceful, rainy run. If I am a hothead, so be it. If I'm deranged, so be it. When I run, I have no tolerance for aggressive stupidity and wanton acts of neglect that put the runner in danger; I feel that by acting solely on immediate, reactive emotions, giving no consideration to rational thought and civilized problem solving, I'm sending a message to discourteous and hoggish drivers that will ultimately benefit not only me, but all those who run, even those who run for the wrong reasons. If they are running, I don't care if they're a jerk. I don't care if they're rich or poor, fat or thin, yuppie or anarchist; they are my brothers and sisters and our brief nods and occasional verbal acknowledgments of each other mask a deeper camaraderie, one which, if acted upon and organized, could potentially end in bloodshed for those who choose to fuck with the runner. I occasionally envision a runner's version of Ballard's *High Rise* in which those who run begin to commit random acts of violence against all drivers, arrogant and rude or not; I would abandon my own car in the middle of the park and set out in my sweatpants and Brooks seeking only to run and devour drivers of vehicles; sinking to a savage, primitive state in which all drivers would be raped, thrashed and ultimately consumed by the higher breed of runners; existing only on a primordial rush of adrenaline and survival; creating a new social order in which drivers of cars and trucks and SUV's and mini-van's are beaten mercilessly; savaged by a society of runners, supreme beings succumbing to the slightest urge to destroy those who would stand in our way. But these are only fantasies, and ones that I realize are presently viewed as demented. Thus, I tend to keep them to myself.

Too many people in this city own dogs. Oak Park is a primarily residential city with a higher-than-average crime rate so I assume most of the dog owners (who must make up at least sixty percent of the population) see their dogs as deterrents against the criminal element. The problem for the runner is two-fold. One, many people don't realize that when walking their dogs, they should use the leash to pull the dog to the side when a runner approaches. I deal with them simply: "To the side, to the side...," I tell them gently but firmly. A much more offensive and potentially dangerous type of owner is the one who lets his dog roam around leash-free.

Dogs don't like me. I was bitten by many dogs as a child, never severely, but often enough to decide that I don't like them either. But dog owners are convinced that THEIR dog is a well-trained, good-natured, obedient canine that would never even consider taking a chunk out of an innocent runner's leg. When I see these unleashed dogs, I immediately scan the area for the owner. Once spotted, I yell, as loudly as possible, "PUT A LEASH ON THAT DOG!" or, if the owner looks particularly offensive or stupid, I'll yell "PUT A LEASH ON THAT FUCKIN' THING BEFORE I CALL THE COPS!" The offenders seldom answer back. What can they say? There IS a leash law in Oak Park and they ARE breaking it. I've only gotten two responses when I've yelled at owners of unleashed dogs. One was from a woman who said, "It's not my dog."

"Then," I said as I passed by, "you won't mind when I call Animal Control to pick up that filthy thing and have it gassed."

The other was from an obviously gay man who, when I yelled, "PUT A LEASH ON THAT THING!" responded in a smarmy tone, "That's not nice."

"Neither is getting bitten by a mangy fleabag," I answered, running backwards so he could see my face, which I hoped looked suitably deranged. "So put a leash on that pooch or I'm gonna hafta take matters into my own hands."

I really don't like dogs.

I don't know why I run, which is strange because I usually know why I do things. I smoked in the past because I saw it as part of my identity; I believed I loved smoking and I feared that I'd become a lost, wandering soul without my beloved cigarettes. After I quit for eighteen months, I realized I'd been fooling myself. I didn't need them; they weren't part of my identity; I only enjoyed perhaps one out of every twenty cigarettes I smoked. When I took it up again (then quit, then took it up again — it's been almost a year now) I knew exactly why. I would find myself in a creative burst, and, trancelike, I would go out and buy a case of beer and a few packs of cigarettes and work work work, chain-smoking and drinking, forgetting to eat, furious with my bladder for causing me to get up to go to the bathroom, and I'd do this for hours until I just wasn't any good anymore. Such a burst occurred late last December. At first, I only smoked in the guest room. Then only in the guest room and my office. Then everywhere. And that's where it stands now.

But while I'm physically addicted to nicotine, I'm not mentally addicted to cigarettes anymore. I'll quit soon enough. I know why I smoke and I know how to quit. And I know why I STARTED running again — to lose weight. I'd ballooned to a wholly unacceptable 180 pounds — the largest I'd ever been. Now I'm down to 157. But I don't continue to run to keep the weight off; the stress of my divorce and adjusting to a bachelor's life that involves a lot of working, little cooking and many missed meals has been sufficient enough to keep me from becoming puffy and large again.

I've discovered something comforting in the routine of running — that's a small part of it — but it's the aloneness of it that I find addictive. It clears my head and it makes me feel clean, mentally and physically. But these aren't logical enough reasons to keep running because they're intangible, and intangibles usually don't provide the motivation necessary to keep me exerting myself; despite all the work I do, I am inherently lazy and generally reluctant to put forth physical effort unless I see immediate results. The truth is, I simply don't know why I run anymore.

The only other thing in which I immerse myself for reasons that have no tangible basis is love. There aren't many downsides to running, aside from the occasional physical injury, like the strain in the muscle just above my right knee that I'm presently nursing. Love has many downsides, but I find it even more addictive than running.

I don't know why I get involved in love, especially when it always ends up badly, if only in the sense that I seldom get what I want. I've been lucky enough to avoid any major catastrophes, but things never quite work out. But I crave love; I long for human contact; the touch of a woman; a kiss; a long embrace; an animalistic fuck; and, like a whipped dog, I keep coming back to females, waiting — as if I don't have a choice (and sometimes I feel as if I really don't) — for that whipped dog to finally get tired of the abuse and turn mean. Love often feels like digging a deep hole and filling it back in, endlessly, twenty-four hours a day. But I get something out of it, something similar to running. It's those occasional moments of feeling freedom combined with a loose control, of vivid perception, of seeing everything click into place and move as if I'm standing outside of myself watching a precisely tuned motor humming along.

But running is solitary; love takes two. So love is more; it's unique; its human-to-human synergy can't be duplicated except in rare situations in music, when working with a band. It's those brief moments of clarity in which everything that you feel can't be summed up but just sits there in a lump somewhere in your throat and it's okay and you don't have to explain it. It's experiencing something with another person that shouldn't be talked about, like watching the sun rise; and you both know it's better to just shut up and watch. It's the perfection of that synergy, an occasional experience of true bliss, a rare glimpse into heaven. These moments are brief but they are pure and they are beautiful and they keep me coming back for more.

I don't love running; I just practice running. Someday I'll learn to stop loving the concept of love. Someday I'll learn to stop wanting and start experiencing and appreciating what I have when I have it, no matter how seemingly insignificant. When I learn to stop looking too deeply into the future, setting goals, imagining what things might be like with the person I love, then I'll finally know how to love correctly, or at least be on the path to understanding it a little better. Someday I'll learn to just practice love.

Until then, I will continue to practice running.

THE INFINITE JOYS OF BEING A PROFESSIONAL MUSICIAN

A lot of young punk musicians have asked me for advice on how to get a record deal. I always tell them to quit playing music. If you try to make a living by playing music, you're destined for a lot of headaches, heartaches and, 999 times out of a thousand, total failure. When we started Screeching Weasel, I try to explain to these eager young men and women, the possibility of making a living from it didn't exist. You could count on one hand the number of active punk bands who earned a living through music, and virtually all of them did so by touring constantly, living with their band members and allowing the band to engulf their entire lives. This is about the point when people stop listening. They don't want to hear about the old days. They only know about Green Day and Blink-182. When we learned, in 1991, that our third album had sold 5,000 copies in the first six months of its release, we were astounded. We had never planned for that type of unprecedented success. To these kids, 5,000 units mean nothing. Less than nothing.

So because they don't understand the mentality that somehow afforded us success — the freedom to do whatever we goddamn well felt like because we had nothing to lose and (we thought) nothing to gain — and because I don't understand their mentality — picking up a microphone or a guitar with ideas of becoming the next big thing — I usually don't bother to go into much detail about the little things I've learned over the past 16 years — things I often learned the hard way — that have helped me to pay the bills with a band that was never anywhere near popular enough to justify "career" status. But at the urging of my publisher and friend, who thinks this stuff might be of interest to some people, as well as my literary agent, who remains slightly deluded regarding the level of the public's interest in my dubious musical career, I present to you some random tidbits that may help you out if you're ever stupid or insane enough to actually invest the necessary time and money into the always cash-hungry monster known as the Punk Rock Band. I direct my comments primarily towards the egomaniacs after my own heart, the shameless, crazed lunatics who have either the balls or lack of brain cells to take the wheel and become the bandleader.

To begin with, don't run your band as a democracy. Before you even agree to work with others in a band, make it clear that you're calling the shots. Democracies don't work in music.

You have to understand that there are two elements to being in a successful band: the creative side and the business side. Neither is more or less important than the other. Slack off on the business end and you'll end up bitter and angry. Put business before art and you'll find yourself coming up with all kinds of creative ways to justify compromises that not only tear at your soul, but that also inevitably affect the quality of your music.

If you play music, especially punk music, for any reasonable length of time, you will soon be called a sell-out. Understand something: If you ever take your songs out of the garage or basement and perform them for money or goods — even if you only get paid five dollars, or even if you sell demo tapes for two and a quarter or as a trade for an old Clash t-shirt — understand that as of that moment you have sold out. You are now a businessman. Punks often get this confused; they think if you're not making money, you're not a businessman. Wrong. If you're not making money, it just means you're a *lousy* businessman, or your product hasn't yet caught on. When you begin, you will find yourself thanking whatever gods may exist that you scored a gig opening for some marginally popular local band in some suburban basement. You won't even expect to get paid. That's fine. When you're starting out, you should take any gigs you can get. But as your popularity grows, you should be setting a price for your services. Even if you're only consistently drawing between 25 and 30 people to a show, multiply that number by your average door price, subtract the promoter's cut, other bands' cut and any soundman fees and use that as your guarantee. Don't play for less, even if it's only twenty bucks.

In our culture, artists are expected to be either obnoxiously wealthy prima donnas or below-the-poverty-line martyrs. There is literally no other business in our society that allows the customer to get something for nothing. Even people who work for excellent, positive, helpful non-profit organizations earn a salary, and they get something you don't — health care benefits. Don't allow yourself to be financially bullied by people who treat you as though you should be entertaining them out of the goodness of your heart. None of those people go through life without roofs over their heads and food in their bellies. They would never consider demanding that a plumber fix their leaky toilet for no charge, or that the Amoco station should be handing out free tanks of gas to prove that they're still doing it for the people. Hell, people who win the lottery through a combination of a .2% investment and 99.8% luck aren't vilified, so why should you be? Playing in a band is very expensive and you need money to operate and if you're good — and you'll know it if people come to see you play — you absolutely deserve to turn a profit. But I'm starting to get a little bit ahead of myself, and I want to shift gears here to talk about art.

Just as you are a businessman, you are also an artist. Conventional punk wisdom says otherwise, but conventional punk wisdom is wrong. When you create music, you become an artist. It doesn't matter if you never sell it, or if you try to sell it and nobody wants to buy it. Music is art. The only degrees involved are based on quality. The person who produces bad art is as much of an artist as the person who produces good art, or mediocre art. Your music may be offensive or difficult to appreciate and those who are offended or confused might scoff and tell you that what you're doing isn't art. They're wrong; it's just art that they don't care for.

Most people involved in art, whether it's music, writing, painting, drawing or whatever, don't feel like artists. This is based on the incorrect assumption that you will feel something special and go through a sudden, eye-opening, world-altering change once you've finally become a real artist. Any changes that you may experience as the result of being in a band have nothing to do with being an artist or not being one. You already are an artist. That doesn't make you any more special than anyone else, but neither does it make you a phony, which is how many artists feel. Because we're not taught anything real about art in this culture, we don't know how to react when people congratulate us on our work, or when they knock it. There is no textbook for how to deal with success and failure as an artist. We just follow along with what we've been taught from watching TV and movies and reading interviews: if you're a newer band with a tiny fanbase, you're supposed to be humble, gracious and deferential, like a 19th-century slave thanking his owner for giving him an extra piece of bread after a day of picking cotton. If you're successful, you're supposed to be a drunk or a drug addict, and you are considered a sell-out no matter what you may do or how you conduct your business. Successful musicians are always subjected to angry scrutiny and if people can't find evidence of actual wrongdoing, they'll condemn you on principle; if you're making a profit, you *must* be doing something evil. Having been both a loud-mouthed jerk who unfairly attacked punk musicians, as well as a musician who has been subjected to such nonsense, I can tell you without reservation that it's all crap. Most music fans do not walk through life chronically offended, but those who do are extremely loud. Try to ignore them. A lot of things get easier as you experience success in music, but there are two things that are very important.

First, the feeling that you're a fraud will eventually go away. Unfortunately for many, an air of superiority, which is, of course, just a front for lingering insecurities, replaces it. But if you can maintain balance, you'll come to realize that what you do musically is unique and of value, while at the same time understanding that you are human, and ultimately just another jerk like the rest of us.

Secondly — and people in all walks of life experience this — the anger and frustration you feel about those who knock you or treat you unfairly — that anger which is not only directed at the people doing the yapping, but at yourself for letting it get to you — will change. Eventually, you *will* stop caring, not all at once, and maybe never 100%, but enough so that cheap shots and unfounded accusations begin to affect you less and less.

Early on in a band, it may be difficult to tell whose creative voice stands out. Often, two or more members will be writing songs. Gradually the dominant voice will become clear. Occasionally, two or more band members will be great songwriters and will contribute to the sound of the band. More often than not, the task will fall to one member. Once that's been determined, you have to be able to handle the inevitable confrontation. If you're so afraid of confrontation (and nobody *likes* it, by the way) that you're willing to let your potentially great band stay mired in mediocrity, then you just don't have the stomach for what lies ahead and you should quit now. There are many potential problems in dealing with the conflict of telling a fellow band member that his or her songs aren't working for your band, but the most common one will be the offending songwriter reciting a list of friends, fans and fanzine reviewers who like his or her songs. This may sound like a persuasive argument but it's actually faulty for two reasons. First, the worst songs in the world will always appeal to somebody. I'm still amazed at the number of people who like some of my worst songs

— songs that I know are bad, and that pretty much everybody else knows are bad. Secondly, punks have an irritating habit of trying to create dissension between band members (this is much easier to do to a smaller band). The soon-to-be-relieved-of-his-duties songwriter will have no problem finding punks to back him up just so they can watch and rub their hands together in glee as your band swirls down the toilet. Be aware of this and make any changes that need to be made without fear of backlash from the scenesters.

Through both experience and observation, I've come to the conclusion that democracy in songwriting generally doesn't work. There are exceptions, but they are rare. Occasional contributions from other members are fine if they write something worthwhile, but for the most part, the creative leader should be writing the songs in order to shape the sound and feel of the band. The saying "too many cooks spoil the broth" is probably more appropriate as a metaphorical case for adherence to a single band member's creative vision than it is as a statement about cooking.

Democracy in the business affairs of the band is something that can turn out messy as well; my advice is to have a limited democracy, i.e. everyone gets a say but the buck stops with the band leader. Often, the creative leader doesn't possess the skills to be the business leader, and even more often he doesn't want both roles (this usually means he wants to make important business decisions but he doesn't want to have to do the dirty work). In my case, I was a control freak. As time went by, I began giving more control to John "Jughead". For one thing, he was loyal. I knew that with his ethics he wouldn't steal from the band, and he had certainly earned my trust to do his best, even if he blew it sometimes. Besides, when I was running the business by myself, I was screwing up on a regular basis — I figured it couldn't get any worse. John also possessed some important qualities in dealing with band business: He was good with numbers, he was frugal, he was willing to put in the necessary work, he learned quickly, and he wouldn't allow himself to be taken advantage of, all qualities which, except for the latter, I didn't possess. I was terrible with numbers, I took forever to learn new concepts and, through equal parts naiveté and laziness, I'd made some awful financial decisions, some of which haunt us to this day. John was not very comfortable with confrontation, so over time we developed a system whereby I would deal with the hard-ass stuff like contract negotiations, booking studio time, and recruiting band members to join our revolving door of musicians, and he dealt with the less glamorous stuff — the little details that scream for attention like paying the bills, writing royalty checks to band members, getting clearance for cover songs, etc. I never had the attention span for the little details and it caused a lot of problems. With John at the helm of the business desk, things worked much more smoothly.

In my band's case, it took two people to do the job. But if you have a band member who is willing and able to deal with your business, allow him room to make mistakes. Running the business of a band is not easy. You'll make it easier if you're not dipping into the till for a peep show when everybody's back is turned, and if you're not coming down on the poor fool every time something goes wrong or a mistake is made. It's a tough, unglamorous job, so cut your business guy some slack.

One of the many things that's changed since 1986 about being in a punk band is that with the rise in popularity of the genre, there's been a radical shift in the way business is done and in how bands conduct themselves. Many of these changes have been good — for instance, bands are a bit more business-savvy than they used to be and probably get taken advantage of less — but good or bad, most of the changes seem to be permanent. Rather than list all the things I miss, and there are many, I'd like to point out some seemingly accepted truths that aren't entirely correct.

Most young bands see getting on a bill — or better yet, a tour — as a supporting act for a more popular band as being a crucial step towards attracting a wider fan base. Though it's true that with more bands than ever out there it's more important to do things that will help you stand out, I don't believe that touring with a popular band is necessary for success. The view that piggybacking is an essential component of getting your band noticed has created a situation in which many great, young bands simply aren't touring at all. They're too busy waiting around at home for some more popular band to ask them to open for them on tour.

Well, if you're sitting around waiting to be invited on a tour, be prepared to wait for a long time. Other bands notice you by seeing you play, and not just once in front of your hometown crowd. If you don't get out and tour on your own, you'll never meet people. Perhaps more importantly, not only will you fail to get the attention of popular bands, but you'll miss out on the much more satisfying experience of meeting people just like you, in bands as unpopular as yours, some of whom will be famous one day. My best memories of being on the road tend to revolve around hanging out with people in towns all over the country who were in the same boat as us. We felt like we were really onto something unique. We didn't lack respect for those who came before us — quite the contrary — but we recognized that what we were doing was *now*. It was our generation, our time and our music, even if nobody cared then and even though many of the older fans still look at us as a joke. And by the way, many of those people we met and became friends with are famous now. It was an amazing experience and there is nothing that has changed so much that you can't experience something similar. There's not a single piggyback band from the 80's that ever really made a name for themselves; if I listed the bands — who indeed benefited slightly in the short term from their unabashed butt-kissing — you wouldn't know who the hell I was talking about.

I'm not trying to tell you that you absolutely shouldn't try to get an opening slot on a popular band's tour. But use your head. If you're not in the same ballpark as them as far as musical styles, you're wasting your time. Don't open for a band whose fans are going to react to you indifferently at best. And even if you get on a tour with a band whose fans might like you, remember that no matter how popular the band is, a good percentage of their fans won't even show up until you've finished your set. Most of the fans will view you as a distraction. You'll most likely make less money than if you went out on a self-booked tour. And on a self-booked tour, you may be playing to a smaller crowd but they'll be there to see you. They will feed you, they will give you a place to sleep and they will never forget you, especially in the small towns. Maybe we're an unusual case, but Screeching Weasel only opened for three bands in our existence. With the possible exception of a sold-out Operation Ivy gig at Gilman Street, those gigs didn't make the slightest bit of difference in our popularity.

Screeching Weasel didn't do a lot of things the way we were supposed to, and it's surprising that we did as well as we did. We never toured for more than six weeks a year and we went long stretches — years — without touring at all. We didn't make t-shirts to sell to fans until our second tour — three years after we formed — and even then we were just buying t-shirts at K-Mart and hitting them with homemade screens. I remember on Jawbreaker's last tour, they ran out of t-shirts. Instead of standing around empty-handed until their merch company could send more shirts out, they went out to a thrift store, bought as many shirts as they could afford, quickly made a makeshift stencil and spray painted "JB" on the shirts. That's the coolest Jawbreaker shirt I own.

Since the mid-90's I've watched young bands selling three different t-shirt designs before they've even released a record. I guess that's fine — we all know that merch is where the money is at gigs — but there is something about it that I find a little cynical. I don't think it's any coincidence that those bands tend to have the look and the attitude down, but can seldom back it up with good songwriting. If today's bands spent half the time learning the art of songwriting that they spend on networking, they'd all be making a lot more money and we'd all be listening to a lot less crap.

Touring sucks. Even when it's fun, it sucks. Being stuck in a van with three band mates for weeks on end is not a healthy situation. More bands I know have broken up during or just after a tour than for any other reason. My band, The Riverdales, did a three-month tour that permanently ruined some friendships and severely damaged others; we just spent entirely too much time in each other's company. If you can tour with your band for a month, come home and blow off some steam and still be able to get along with and basically like your band mates, hold onto them. Touring makes men out of boys. Hell, touring makes men out of girls.

I've known some bands that can go out on the road, party like crazy, miss gigs, play sloppy, drunken sets that leave crowds feeling bored and ripped off and still continue to grow in popularity. The vast majority of them don't last very long. Even for a young, strong, energy-filled teenager, touring quickly takes its toll. It is not an easy life when you're sober and it becomes harder when you're loaded. It's a physically and emotionally exhausting, frustration-laden, anxiety-filled experience. Gigs get cancelled, promoters duck out without paying you or they skim from the door and then surround themselves with goons to discourage you from asking for a recount, drunks challenge you to fights and cops pull your van over for carrying a bunch of weird-looking creeps. You get drunk and screw an attractive female fan only to wake up sober with a deranged stalker on your hands. You're ready to leave on a night drive because your next gig is 500 miles away and your drummer is off somewhere getting head from a barmaid. You stop talking to your bassist, except for the occasional "fuck off" and you talk shit about the other band members with your drummer while they're eating at a separate table. Then when you eat with them, you talk shit about your drummer. Kid promoters decide at the last minute that they want to add another band to a bill on which six are already playing. You've got a 300-mile drive and another band will put you off to a 2 a.m. start so you stand firm. If you're lucky, the neglected band just calls you assholes and writes letters to fanzines about what stuck-up rock stars you are. If you're unlucky, you start loading out your gear only to discover that your van's tires have been slashed. Drunken yahoos decide it would be fun to throw beer bottles at your head on stage. You find yourself on the verge of tears as yet another absolutely horrible local band gets up to play a 75 minute set while you wait to play and get the hell out before you strangle somebody. You blow your ears and vocal chords out singing through an ancient P.A. with no stage monitors while standing in puddles of spit, beer and puke. If you can get through all that and still have the desire to go out on the road again, you might be stupid enough to be able take this band stuff to the next level.

Another common misconception courtesy of the rise in popularity of punk music is that you need a manager, roadie, soundman and road manager if you're going to take your band seriously. If nobody in your band has any business sense, you may well need a manager and a road manager. But you need to be making money in order to be successful enough to afford to pay those cats, and you're probably not going to make any money if you don't have any business sense. We had a road manager when I was with the Riverdales and we were opening for Green Day in Europe. It was a very nice luxury, as was having a driver and a roadie. But then, we lost $30,000 on that tour. We eventually made the money back through record sales, but it's interesting that the only "professional" tour I've done was also the only one I've done where the band came home more than $200 in debt.

Having a soundman that tours with you is great, or so I've been told. The Riverdales sort of had one when we toured with Green Day; their monitor guys ran our sound and monitors, and their lighting guys did our lights as well. (This is by no means common courtesy for a major label act. Green Day knew we were not in a financial position to tour with all those luxuries and they looked out for us. They not only provided us with sound and lights free of charge, but they carried our gear in their truck — which was loaded in and out by their gem of a stage manager/roadie, Tim Chunks — and occasionally would refuse to give interviews unless the press interviewed us as well. Green Day were extremely good to us both professionally and personally — they even took up for us, very loudly, when their idiotic, long-since-fired road manager was giving us shit. But be advised that this is not common behavior for major label acts — if you go on tour with a typical major label act you might actually run into them two or three times on the entire tour.). Dealing with a club soundman can be horrible; many of these guys are bitter, failed musicians who deeply resent having to work for bands who are out there doing what they never could. But being cooperative and courteous can go a long way towards forging a brief, successful relationship with a soundman — many of them are good people who are really trying to do the best job they can — and until you can really afford to bring your own soundman on the road, learn how to take a break from your sound check while the rest of the band is still playing to walk around the venue and check things out. Make your requests to the soundmen politely. You catch more flies with honey.

Roadies are another luxury. A good roadie is gold. I've been lucky enough to work with two different roadies who were both outstanding. But we didn't hire our first roadie until after our fourth album was released. We seldom hired merch people and I only went on the road with one twice — both times with the Riverdales.

A good roadie doesn't want you touching your gear while it's being loaded and unloaded. He has a system and he doesn't want you screwing it up. He can drive for at least an eight-hour stretch. He will take the punches from drunken imbeciles that were intended for you and he's tough enough to tame them. He can change a guitar string at lightning speed and he catches falling mike stands and toppling amps before they can hit the stage. He is your muscle when dealing with a rip-off promoter. He never gets involved in band arguments and certainly never takes sides. He is always exactly where he's supposed to be when he's supposed to be there. He is superhuman. You cannot pay him enough money. Budget a large salary for him and give him bonuses. He does the absolute shittiest work in the business of punk rock and he puts up with your silly rock star bullshit and he does it with a grim determination and unquestionable loyalty. Ignore the common roadie penchant for S&M — what he does in the privacy of the loft of the van is his own business. Pay him well and thank him profusely because once you've worked with a good roadie, you will never again be able to work properly without him.

I suppose I should write a long section detailing how to get signed to a record label. That's what everyone wants. They think that once they get signed most, if not all of their problems will be over. Wrong. Your problems are just beginning. As for how to get signed to a record label, it's not that difficult, especially these days when there are so many labels around. Sending a demo tape or CD to the label will likely get you nothing. If you're lucky, the mail order guy or girl might give a listen to the first thirty seconds of the first song before tossing it in the trash, but most of the time the mail order people are too busy for such antics. If you want to get signed, play. Tour. Repeat, over and over and over. If you're good, somebody will notice you and offer you the coveted blessing/curse — the record contract.

Don't screw around with small time labels. They can't do anything for you that you can't do for yourself. If a small label with limited distribution (they'll always tell you their distribution is great but if it that were true, they wouldn't be a small label) offers you a small advance to make a record, turn it down. Play gigs, take on extra hours at your job and sell blood to come up with the money to record and manufacture your record or CD yourself. Don't get me wrong — it's a nightmare. Finding a good, competitively-priced manufacturer, getting the art laid out and sized correctly, dealing with distributors who pay you late or not at all—these are only some of the pitfalls of releasing your own stuff. And you'll probably make it worse by getting friends to help you. Your drummer will know somebody who does graphic design. She's offering to lay out your CD for free. You'll be thrilled until you have to deal with the printing company telling you how much it's going to cost for them to fix all of her mistakes if you want to get it released within the next three years. Unless these friends have plenty of experience specifically working on CD's or records, politely decline.

A small label will get your records into some stores, but you'll sell more copies and get your money quicker if you sell as many as possible at gigs and through mail order. Yes, it's a pain in the ass, but some of the nicest people I ever met agreed to do a record because they were a "fan of the band" only to take our master tapes and proceed to flake out or rip us off in too many ways to go into. Tapes get lost or stolen, the labels press and sell more than they agreed to and don't pay you the extra money, and you can never get in touch with them. When you finally do get more popular and sign to a larger label and want to re-release your old stuff, you'll often find that these nice guys who were only "helping you out" because they were such big fans suddenly decide that they own all the rights to a release that they originally agreed to simply license for a thousand copies. Your label won't want to pay them (and the money they paid would come out of your advance anyway) and you'll want to beat the shit out of them. I've been ripped off plenty and the worst thieves were the guys who waved the D.I.Y., underdog, I'm-just-doing-this-because-I-love-the-music flag. The people who made no bones about being in business have generally treated me right. That doesn't mean all bigger labels are good. In fact, most of them will try to get you to sign horrible contracts that you'll regret for the rest of your life. I know of a label that has signed many popular bands and paid them such a pitiful, nigh-criminal royalty rate that it would be laughable if it weren't so goddamned evil. You buy those records and you have no idea how poorly the bands are treated and how little of the money you spend actually ever gets into the hands of the band members. But beware of the people who come to you with big smiles and open arms. They're often just waiting for you to turn your back.

If you insist on dealing with a small label, at least make sure the label is based in your town, or a reasonable drive away. Though I wouldn't recommend violence as a course of action, a face-to-face confrontation with a label owner who's screwing you can change the tone of your conversations considerably in comparison to a phone call to a guy who's a thousand miles away.

There is a semi-legendary story in Chicago about a well-known underground musician whose band was being ripped off by a fairly large New York label. He finally reached the end of his rope in trying to deal with them on normal human terms and flew to New York. When the label's employees arrived at work the next morning, they were greeted by an angry musician wielding a crowbar. He left shortly after with his master tapes. I have no idea if this story is true or not and I have chosen not to investigate it, because I really want to believe it.

The small label owner who rips you off is a petty thief. He probably makes less money stealing from you than a bootlegger would (though many of these guys also deal in bootlegs). The larger labels generally don't engage in outright stealing. They just take advantage of your ignorance, your eagerness to be signed by a big label and your lack of funds for legal representation to get you to sign contracts that put money that should rightfully be yours into their pockets. It's all legal and once you've signed, you're fucked. Please be advised that the information I offer below is based solely on my personal experience. It will not necessarily be current by the time you read this and although I've had a decent amount of experience in dealing with record contracts, I may well be a little off on some of my information. Use this as a guideline, not as a substitute for common sense or legal advice.

Before you sign the contract, before you even record your album, set up a royalty split with your bandmates. Many bands split royalties evenly and that's fine. Just make sure that if you do so, you won't end up feeling resentful for receiving the same rate as everyone else even though you are doing all the work that would normally be done by a manager. Unless you're going to pay out mechanical (songwriting) royalties directly to the songwriters, make sure to cut the songwriters a higher percentage. And make sure to set aside a percentage of the royalties and/or gig money for business expenses (long distance alone can get pretty pricey when your band goes from part-time hobby to full-time gig). Even when you're just starting out, make sure to get reimbursed for your expenses. Keep receipts and copies of bills. Even if it takes years to get your money back, you won't feel so resentful about all that money you put into the band when the other people in the band weren't contributing.

When discussing royalty splits with band members, lay down what you think is fair and then give them a few weeks to think about it. Be willing to compromise but don't allow yourself to be taken advantage of. And when everyone is agreed on the split, write up a short agreement noting who gets paid what and have each member sign an original that they can keep. And have everybody sign an extra one that you can keep on file and copy to send to the label if they're paying each member individually.

To begin with, you'll be looking for the royalty rate. You get a percentage of the SRLP (Suggested Retail List Price). Don't sign yet. Do the math. As of January of 2002 an average SRLP for a punk rock CD is between $12.98 and $16.98. But before you go working out percentages on your calculator, don't forget the mechanical royalty. When a record label releases an album, or even just one song, they need to obtain a mechanical license from the song publisher for each song. Unless you've signed a publishing deal with someone (and you likely haven't), the publisher is you, the songwriter. The contract will ask for a mechanical license for each song. The industry standard is an offer of 75% of the current statutory rate (the rate at the time you sign the agreement) for a mechanical license on no more than ten songs. This is fair; if labels didn't stop it at ten songs, you could fleece them by recording as many short little songs as possible to cram on a CD and they'd go broke. As of January 1st, 2002, the statutory rate for mechanical licenses is 8 cents per song. As of January 1st, 2004, it will go up to 8.5 cents per song. As of January 1, 2006, it will go up to 9.1 cents per song (these rates are based on songs that are five minutes or less in length). You are locked into the rate that is in effect when you sign the agreement; your rate doesn't change when the overall rate changes. The Harry Fox Agency, a sort of clearinghouse for music publishers that makes sure its members get paid what they're owed, has a Web site that contains current information about the rates (this is also an excellent place to go to begin the process of obtaining the license and negotiating a reduced rate if you want to cover a song — a whole lot of published songs are in the hands of Harry Fox.).

So let's say you're signing a contract for a 14-song album. The mechanical royalty rate is 8 cents per song. 75% of that is 6 cents per song. At a maximum of ten songs, that's 60 cents per unit. Now let's say you get offered nine points (i.e. nine percent of the SRLP) on an album that will list at $13.98 (this figure won't be quoted in the contract because prices change — it may go up, or, if you flop and the label is trying to unload your release, it may go down — simply ask at what price the label is going to list your album). Rounding up, nine percent of $13.98 is $1.26. Add your mechanicals and you're getting $1.86 per unit. In my opinion, that's a criminally low rate for an album. For a young band releasing their first album, that total should be no less than $2.15 per CD (for vinyl, I'll leave it to the reader to get the SRLP and do the math.).

Some contracts contain language stating that the mechanicals will be inclusive in the total royalty. There's nothing wrong with this; just make sure that the total is fair when you do the math. Some truly sleazy labels will ask you to sign away the rights to your mechanicals. The only reason they dare to try to pull such crooked nonsense is because they assume you won't know what mechanicals are. When you ask, they'll tell you that it amounts to mere pennies (technically, a million bucks just amounts to pennies, too) and that it's no big deal. Sometimes they'll just lie and tell you that waiving the rights to your mechanical royalties is standard practice in the record business. Now you know better. Never sign away the rights to your mechanicals.

Technically speaking, you are supposed to receive mechanicals on every unit pressed, whether it's sold or used as promo. Most labels will ask you to sign a contract that will pay you only half the mechanicals on those units used for promotional purposes. I think this is fine and absolutely fair. Some labels will ask you to waive the rights to those mechanicals. I don't think that's fair, though if the rest of the agreement can be worked out so that you're getting a really great deal overall, you might agree to that.

A quick aside: a lot of bands are unsure what to do about dividing up mechanical royalties. Some bands pay them to the songwriters only. Other bands divvy them up. Since all of our agreements are for royalty rates with mechanicals inclusive of the total rate, I never singled out songwriting money as mine. Rather, we divided the total royalty based on seniority, the amount of work the member does for the band, and songwriting. I'm not saying that's the only correct way to do it, but it seems to have worked well for us. I've had ex-band members complain about me for a lot of things, but I'm proud to say that nobody's ever accused me of screwing them on a royalty split. And now I've probably jinxed myself...

Some labels want half of your publishing money. When you join up with BMI or ASCAP (and you should), you fill out a form for every song you've written that's been released, or is about to be released. You need to sign up with either ASCAP or BMI (in Canada you would use

SOCAN) as both a songwriter and publisher. Our publishing company is Weasels, Inc., so named because we already had that business set up as a corporation in 1993 and it didn't require us to set up another business. When you're starting out, you'll need to set up a DBA ("doing business as") and get a bank account in that name (the bank will usually direct you to the County Clerk's office to pay the fees and fill out the proper forms) but for us, using our existing name was easier. By the way, don't worry about setting up your band as a corporation or a limited partnership or anything. When you're making some money you'll need an accountant and he or she will tell you what to do. My experience with our accountant has been good. John deals with him exclusively now as I am not involved in that end of the business, but early on I learned that the best thing you can do when dealing with an accountant is shut up and listen and do what he tells you to do. A good accountant can save you a lot of money.

BMI, ASCAP, SOCAN and other publishing societies charge a nominal fee to become and remain a member. Their job is to collect money for you every time one of your songs is played on a radio station, in a commercial, before the face off at a hockey game, when another band covers your song in a club, whatever (just think about how much money "Blitzkrieg Bop" has brought in. And sadly, songs such as "Born to Be Wild" too…). Naturally, they can't and don't monitor every single radio station and venue in the world. And BMI is much better for punk bands because they do a far better job of monitoring college radio. The only reason we went with ASCAP was because the forms to join these groups are so difficult to figure out and BMI wouldn't help walk me through it. ASCAP has a Chicago office and they were willing to send their guy out to lunch with us to walk us through the process. Whichever way you go, do it. It is essentially free money and I still occasionally kick myself for declaring in 1987 that I wanted no part of that "major label bullshit", and for being too dumb in the early 90's to take the time to try to figure the whole thing out.

Before you ever sign to a label you should already be hooked up with ASCAP or BMI (or SOCAN for the oft-forgotten Canucks). Most labels are going to ask for fifty percent of your publishing for the songs on your release. I've never given it to any label and I never will. Running a record label is a tough business — I know because John and I did it for five non-consecutive years. Good labels deserve to turn a profit. But even with all their overhead, they are still turning a bigger profit than you with your overhead. They did not write your songs, you did. I don't believe they're entitled to my money for songs I wrote and I don't believe they're entitled to yours. It's standard industry practice but I think it stinks and I've never given in to it. If you don't have any leverage (i.e. if you're not very popular yet), you may have to do it, but do so while complaining and holding your nose.

Another common industry practice is to ask for half of any money you may get if one of your songs from the release is used in something like a movie or a TV commercial. I don't have a problem with this. The label has worked to promote your release and has helped to get it heard. If a request comes in to use your song, it's going to come in to the record label. Typically, they'll ask for the Master Use license while you'll retain the Synchronization license. And typically the deal will be structured so that the fee for both those licenses is the same amount, hence the 50%. If the movie is a hit and you haven't signed away half your publishing, you'll make a nice little chunk of change whenever the movie plays on cable TV. (And maybe even if it's not a hit, as was the case with "Angus," a truly wretched excuse for a film which features a Riverdales song and which plays frequently on the TBS Superstation, bringing in a few bucks for me and Vapid a couple of times a year).

If a soundtrack album is released with the movie, you would split the royalty with your label. They may ask you to split the mechanical as well. I think that's fair; again they've done a lot of the work that's gotten Hollywood to notice you.

There are many other intricacies of record contracts I could get into but I only want to concentrate on things that your average entertainment lawyer who is used to dealing with major labels (or indies styled after major labels) wouldn't take offense to, but which you, as an independent musician, should. And the last of these is options.

When you sign with a bigger label, you'll almost always be handed a contract that includes a clause with an option for at least one more release. In other words, your next album is theirs, even though it's not yet even been recorded, or probably even written. As a musician, I hate the idea of options, but as a former label owner, I understand the label's desire for them. I don't know about you, but I don't like being dumped for a more attractive guy. Especially if I paid for the chick's nose job and liposuction. That's essentially what an option is about. If your record flops, the label that has an option for your next release can hope that your next record will do better than the first one and they'll make some of their money back. Or, because it is the label's option, they can cut you loose. If the record does well, the label deserves some of the credit. No, they didn't name your band or write your songs or sit in a van with you having to smell your guitarist's beer farts, but they helped you sell more records than you could have sold on your own or with a smaller label. An ideal relationship (and granted, it's rare) between a band and a label is one in which each side feels like the other has helped them out. By exercising an option on a popular band, the label not only makes money from the next release, but they get the prestige of having a popular band on their label, which will attract more potentially successful bands.

Often labels will try to get an option for multiple releases. I find this ridiculous. It's standard practice for a major label to sign a band to a deal with an option for four or five more releases, but I think it's insanity, particularly for independent labels. If the label won't back down on the option, fine, but if they want more than one additional record, fight 'em on it.

I've never signed for an option with a record deal, excepting a back-dated agreement with Lookout that covered already-released records. Keep in mind though, that by the time the business of punk changed, I was in a position where I had enough clout to refuse to do things like sign away my publishing or agree to options. Young bands don't have that clout and that's why my last point about contracts is important.

Get a lawyer. Yes, they suck. Yes, they cost an outrageous amount of money. Yes, they sit around on the phone with the other guy's lawyer comparing golf handicaps and talking about basketball (I think all lawyers like basketball) while billing you for that time at a rate of about 3 and a half bucks a minute. You can't stop the bleeding but you can slow it.

First, do not under any circumstances use a family or friend connection who is not an entertainment lawyer. Only hire a lawyer who is experienced in dealing with record contracts. Ask him who he has worked for in the past. Your best bet is to get a reference from somebody in a band, but if you can't, choose carefully. Tell him that you want a monthly statement. They'll send you one anyway but you'll sound like you sort of know what the hell you're talking about.

Most importantly, do as much work as possible on your own. Do all negotiating with the label. The lawyer should only be used to cross the I's and dot the T's. You probably won't cover everything but deal with as many issues as possible directly with your label contact. If the label won't negotiate with you and they only want to do it through lawyers, don't do the deal. They know you don't have much money. They're hoping that you'll get tired of writing checks to your lawyer and just cave in and sign. Any big indie label contract is going to have a paragraph in it, usually at the end and sometimes in all capital letters, stating that you, the band, have been advised to seek legal counsel in regards to the contract. So if you decide to sue someday, you can't walk into court and be taken seriously when you say you didn't understand what you were getting yourself into, even if you really didn't.

For a good entertainment lawyer, expect to pay in the neighborhood of $200-$250 an hour. Even doing a lot of the work on your own, you can pay 2-3 grand to negotiate a simple indie label contract. Make conversations as brief as possible — that phone time will kill you. If you let them, lawyers will turn a 5-minute conversation into a 30-minute one. My favorite line to get off the phone with these guys is "Hey, I gotta go take a shit." That always gets rid of them, especially if they just ate lunch.

Don't let them mail or fax you anything. Go pick it up at their office. If you've negotiated a point with the label and your lawyer is explaining the 589 ways it could come back to haunt you, tell him you've made up your mind and you don't want to hear any more about it. You can't let these guys push you around, and they'll try. The best way to deal with them is to do your homework, then play dumb and see if they take the bait. When they do, hit 'em with a couple of facts. They'll always congratulate you on your keen understanding of the world of record contracts. Pretend that you buy their insincere bullshit. They'll still think you're an idiot but they'll be more careful. If they bully you, give them a reality check. I once had a lawyer we'd hired call me at 9:00 on a Saturday morning about some moronic, pointless non-issue. He was very insistent about the exact phrasing of some essentially meaningless little clause in a contract. It got to the point where he raised his voice and swore. I yelled, "Don't you ever fucking yell at me, motherfucker! *I* pay *you* and you better not ever fucking forget it!" He immediately started backpedaling and apologizing and making excuses for his outburst — something about a tough week and a sick kid or some bullshit. I tell you that story not only to impress you with the vision of an unshaven, tattooed, barely-graduated-high school punk rock singer humbling a fancy-pants hot-shot attorney, but also to remind you to always remember that these guys work for you, even if they often try to make it out to be the other way around.

The last of the really boring stuff has to do with copyrights. Copyrights have always confused me and the whole thing seems to have gotten more confusing over the past five or six years.

Technically, once you write a song, it's copyrighted. You own it. But what if somebody steals it? Where's your proof? You need to register with the Library Of Congress. There are two basic forms for your needs as a songwriter. Form PA covers the actual song. Form SR covers the sound recording (CD or record). If you release the album yourself, form SR will cover both the sound recording and the songs; you won't need to fill out both forms. Most labels want both the copyrights. Look on any major label release and you see a © and a circle "p" with the year of release and the label name behind it. Look on almost any Screeching Weasel release and you'll see the © with either Weasels, Inc, No Budget productions or my real name behind it, and the label name behind the circle "p". As far as I know, this just signifies the difference between the owner of the songs and the owner of the songs as a whole as they make up the record. You can go record the song for another album (though most contracts prevent you from doing so for a certain number of years, and from ever doing it with all the songs — rightfully so, I might add) but you cannot release or sell that particular recording of that song to anyone else.

I've asked every label owner and entertainment lawyer I've ever met just exactly how copyrights for music work. Nobody has ever been able to give me a definitive answer and they will occasionally say, "nobody really knows."

The form is easy to fill out. Forms PA and SR are almost identical. If you're not using your real name, make sure to write your real name in the author and/or composer space followed by "whose pseudonym is…" and whatever your punk band name happens to be. What didn't use to be a problem and became one after a shake-up at the copyright office in the mid-90's is registering songs on one form that were written by more than one person. The fee for submitting the form and obtaining registration isn't expensive but multiple forms for one album can get pricey. Beginning in the mid-90's every form I sent in required follow-ups. I'd get letters or phone calls from the copyright office telling me what I needed to change and what new forms I needed to fill out and it became a huge pain in the ass. Filling out the forms is still the one process of making and releasing an album that I dread but it can save you a lot of problems if things ever turn ugly and end up in court.

I want to discuss equipment before I get into recording. High-quality gear is terrific. I have a hot-rodded Mosrite that is the most beautiful looking, best feeling, easiest-playing guitar I've ever picked up. I have a ballsy Marshall JCM 800 modified amp that sits atop a 4x12 Marshall cabinet. And by the way, that's all you need. When you see those big rock bands with six amps and eight, ten, or twenty Marshall cabs up on stage, it's all for show. The on-stage monitor sound is so good it's unnecessary for hearing purposes; in fact, most of the time the amps aren't even plugged in to the majority of the extra cabs. Bands with unnecessary gear are overcompensating. And it doesn't even look cool, unless you're an equipment freak. It's Spinal Tap stuff and it should be left to metal bands.

My Mosrite was fitted with Sperzel locking tuners and two DiMarzio Super 2 pickups. Those were both for practical reasons. Locking tuners help your guitar stay in tune. They're an excellent investment for the touring and recording guitarist. Standard Mosrite pickups are made to get the standard Mosrite surf-rock sound. They don't work too well for punk and they have a microphonic effect that causes feedback, feedback that becomes unbearable in a small practice room. A lot of people have asked me why I bothered to pay so much money for a guitar like that only to turn around and drastically alter its sound. It's for the same reason I bought a Floyd Rose Stratocaster and immediately stripped it of its Floyd Rose tremolo bar — I love the feel of the guitar. The Floyd Rose model seems to have a slightly thinner neck than a standard Strat — that's crucial for a guy who has zero flexibility on his fingers. I generally don't like Strats as I find them to be hard to play and prone to a lot of electrical problems. I really love the Gibson Les Paul but those things are so heavy that they're not much fun to strap around your shoulder and lug around on a stage. The Mosrite is a great combination of the feel of a Gibson neck and the body of a Strat. As a bonus, the Mosrite rings almost as loud as an acoustic guitar when I play it so I can write songs at 3 a.m. (which I often do, stumbling into the office half-awake from a dream song I've just written subconsciously) without waking the neighbors. The new Mosrites have the strings set closer to the pickups so they don't produce that wonderful effect. When my pal Flav at guitarpunk.com did a limited edition of a Mosrite copy called the Weaselrite I made sure the bridge was set up properly. Consider it my small effort to control noise pollution.

I think my songwriting has improved dramatically over the past 17 years that I've been writing, but it has nothing to do with guitars. I started out at age 17 on a "K" guitar, an ugly little sunburst thing with little flowers stenciled on the pick guard that I got for $30 from my neighbor, who threw in a cheap, plastic practice amp.

By 1988 I was playing a Hondo, purchased along with a slightly better practice amp for a total of $100. The Hondo was my only guitar for four years. I always recommend that guitarists keep a backup on stage to keep things moving along if a string breaks but I never needed a backup with the Hondo. If I broke a string I'd finish the set as best I could. And it rarely went out of tune. That guitar was indestructible. I was playing rhythm guitar for the Vindictives once at a small anarchist coffee house with one outlet in the room, which of course wasn't grounded. I'm no electrical expert, but I learned a long time ago that if your power isn't grounded, your mike shocks the hell out of you every time your lips touch it. I was playing and singing backups on the wobbly stage, trying to keep as much distance as possible between my mouth and the mike but I kept getting zapped. At the end of the set I was so pissed off that I turned around and threw the Hondo as hard as I could against a cinder block wall about six feet away. The entire back of the guitar landed flush against the wall before flopping over on the strings. My band mates cringed. I threw it in the case and brought it home, making plans to try to get in some extra hours at work for a new guitar. A few days later I pulled it out. There wasn't a scratch on it and it was still perfectly in tune. That thing was a rock. I hate guys who get goofy over guitars but I really developed a sentimental attachment to the Hondo after that. I auctioned it off for $600 a few years ago and I still regret it.

 An Epiphone SG replaced the Hondo in 1992. I immediately loved that guitar. It looked cool and it fit right. I kept the cheap pickups in it and used it almost exclusively for two years (the Hondo became my backup). I kept breaking one of the strings — it would break very easily and always down near the bridge. I learned that this is a common problem with SG's. The cheap bridges sometimes have tiny, almost microscopic burrs where the strings sit, so when you play, your strings get cut every time you strum it. Mass Giorgini gave me a couple of hints on how to fix it, if you can't afford a higher-quality graphite bridge, which I recommend to anyone who's had this problem. Take off the offending string and run the tip of a pencil in and out of the groove. That usually fixes the problem. If that doesn't work, get a fine piece of sandpaper, fold it up and give it a few swipes. I also got some tips on how to keep the guitar in tune better. I couldn't afford locking tuners, which go a long way towards helping, but the simple act of stretching the strings as you put them on one by one helps quite a bit. Some people give them a few cursory tugs, but when I re-string my guitar, I'll spend at least twenty minutes stretching them out. You may want to wear a light pair of gloves while doing this — it starts to really cut into your palms and fingers after a while. The easiest thing you can do to help keep guitars in tune is to play a heavier-gauge string. 9 gauge strings are okay for studio work when you're recording solos that require a lot of string bending, but if you're primarily playing rhythm tracks, you should be using at least 10 gauge strings. I use 11 gauge strings and have been doing so since about 1988. If you're used to a lighter string it will take some getting used to, but I've found the heavier strings easier to play. As a bonus, they don't break as easily.

In 1994 I got a couple of Mosrites. I sold one — the '68 — a few years ago, but I've held on to the main one. I still have the Epiphone though I'm planning on selling it soon, and I still have the Strat, which I'm also going to sell, plus three Weaselrites, two of which have never been played. That's a lot of guitars for a guy who can't play a chord and barely ever touches a guitar.

For the first few years we were together, we were all on the cheap equipment-wise. John played a Westone guitar that would not stay in tune through a tiny Peavey practice amp hooked up to a large stereo speaker. Whoever was playing bass for us played the Screeching Weasel bass — an ugly red Yamaha owned by John that was handed down to several bass players until it was stolen from our practice space in 1992. That bass was played exclusively through John's little Yamaha guitar amp. We were laughed at, mostly affectionately, for coming on stage with our itty-bitty amps, but it was okay. It contributed greatly to the high-end sound of the band, a sound that was completely unintentional. In fact, we were forever trying to get a more low-end sound to our gear. Buying real amps was out of the question — there was no money for such extravagances.

Eventually, we grew attached to our little set up. When the producers looked down their noses at us as we set up our gear to record *My Brain Hurts*, we were coldly defiant. We spurned offers to use the studio's big, powerful Marshall and Mesa Boogie amps. We didn't need all those trappings. We had our shitty gear and we were proud of it.

By the time we recorded our next album, we'd gotten better equipment. *My Brain Hurts* had made money and John and I are not the types to hold onto an inferior set up when we can afford better. We'd also learned that we'd have to get better gear to get the sound we wanted.

When the band ended, John was playing an SG through a Marshall JCM-900 SLX (he smashed his backup SG into tiny little pieces at the end of our last gig), Mass was playing a Fender Precision bass through a Gallien Krueger amp, Phillip was playing my Weaselrite prototype through my JCM 800 and Lumley was playing a killer set of Premier drums that he's had for years. Sometimes I miss the old days when we had our wee gear and shitty guitars and I sang into a Radio Shack microphone duct taped to a broom handle that rested on the basement floor in a bucket. We had no P.A. until 1992; prior to that I sang through a practice amp.

A quick note about singing, and take it with a grain of salt because I don't sing correctly (the correct way is to sing from your diaphragm, not from your throat and head). In the course of recording, you will get advice from people on the proper way to sing. While singing from your belly is easier on your voice, it's harder to master than just yelling out the tunes. If you can do it, fine, but plenty of great singers don't. Henry Rollins is an example of a singer who sings from his diaphragm. He has a strong, powerful, well-controlled voice. Jets To Brazil's Blake Schwarzenbach may have changed his style now, but for years, he sang from the head.

For many years, I thought that the proper way to sing was to tilt your head up towards the mike. A recording engineer told me that singing that way makes it easier to sing from your diaphragm, and provides a more natural passage for air and sound. But a couple of years ago, I mentioned this to my neighbor, who is a tenor in Chicago's Lyric Opera. He told me it was nonsense; he claimed that singers all have different styles and that it depends entirely on the individual. I believe him. Sing in a way that feels right to you, not how somebody says you should.

If you can afford nice gear, get it. Get that dream guitar and that ripping amp. Go take singing lessons if you can stomach the thought. But don't ever think you need that stuff to start a band. You need good tunes. Any guitar and amp will do. The only necessity outside of that is electricity.

I hate rehearsing; I've hated it for ten years. It's gotten easier as I've worked with better and better musicians who don't require my presence as much but I still feel about as good about going to band practice as I do about going in to have a cavity filled.

I feel the opposite about recording. I used to despise it. I hated how long it took — even in the days when we were doing entire 27-song albums in an evening and mixing the whole thing 24 hours later. Recording vocals is still an irritation, but it's minor. I'm still frustrated by the limitations of my voice but I've learned how to write songs that don't demand too much of me vocally. I can't play guitar for shit and my singing isn't much better but I do have musical talent — I can write songs. If I had it my way, I would've given up recording music years ago in favor of writing songs for other bands. Unfortunately punk rock seldom works that way; people get awfully uptight about recording songs written by their contemporaries.

I'm not very interested in the way things work. If something breaks down in my apartment, I seldom attempt to fix it myself. If you're like me, you know how frustrating it is not to be able to fix a toilet or a leaky faucet. When I blew a circuit breaker a few weeks ago I had to have my buddy Chris — a professional contractor — come down and put the new one in for me. It's a very simple process but with my limited ability and knack for fucking things up, I'm sure I would've electrocuted myself or set the building on fire.

But for some reason, I've taken a slight interest in some aspects of recording, especially the stuff that makes life easier without ruining the spontaneity. I really like singing a song five times in a row on five different tracks and then mixing and matching the best parts. It's much better than the old days when I would have to try to sing the same parts over and over until I either got them right (which was rare) or give up and say, resigned, "That's a take."

I love click tracks, too. A click track, if you don't know, is just a sample, like from a drum machine, to help you keep time like a metronome. It gets pumped into your headphones. It's primarily for the drummer, though it can help guitarists and singers who are dealing with breaks in the song and whatnot. I never use it when I'm doing vocals because I find it distracting — it's hard for me to sing with conviction when there's an unnatural clicking in my ears. Some drummers — and it has nothing to do with how good they are — simply can't work with a click. If they're good enough, they won't need to, but I've found that the best drummers prefer it. Click tracks can be a problem, though. If you find yourself getting so hung up on keeping in perfect time with the click track that it's destroying the spontaneity of your performance, drop it. Clicks should only be used with really outstanding musicians who can nail songs in a few takes.

I'm not very picky about drums. I don't like to bother with miking the snare on the bottom because whenever you do that you never end up using the bottom mike anyway. I do have a definite preference for a snare sound though and I've never quite nailed it exactly the way I want it, though we came close on *Teen Punks In Heat*.

I wouldn't say that I've gone full-circle in recording, but I've certainly learned some lessons the hard way. Our first two albums were recorded for $1,000 and $2,000 respectively. We later re-mixed the second album for the British licensing and that cost us about $600. *My Brain Hurts* was done for about $750, though we got a huge break on the recording bill — I believe it took nine days to finish, largely because I was too busy working on ways to get us home from California due to a dead van to be in the studio keeping things moving.

Since then, we've averaged $5-6000 per album, including mixing and mastering. We've spent much more and much less, but roughly eight days and around $5,000 seems to work well for me.

Before I move on and finally end this piece, I want to mention some basics if you've done little or no studio work.

First, show up prepared. Make sure you're well rehearsed. Don't enter the studio with lyrics half-finished or no ending to a song. Studios are expensive; it's much cheaper to work out the kinks in your practice room.

Bring your guitars in to a professional to have the intonation set before you record. Many guitar shops have people who will do this for a reasonable fee. Anything that's going to go wrong will go wrong in the studio, not in your practice room. If you can manage it, bring backup guitars in case one of them goes goofy with intonation problems. Try to bring backup amps as well. Don't spend too much time trying to fix an equipment problem — if it can't be fixed in twenty minutes, reach for the backup.

Drummers should put new skins on at least a few days before recording. Beat on 'em at a few rehearsals to break 'em in. If your drummer doesn't know how to tune his drums, get a tech who can do it before you start getting drum sounds in the studio.

Recording studios make money by recording bands. They also make a lot of money providing a playpen for people who would rather goof around than work. It's your money, spend it wisely.

If you're not working, stay out of the control room unless you can keep your mouth shut. Engineers want your business so they are not going to tell you to keep quiet. You'll find out the hard way — through your album, which won't be recorded as well as it could've been because the engineer wasn't able to fully concentrate on the recording.

Recording engineers have heard every cornball cliché in the book. They don't want to hear you proclaim in a bad British accent that your amps go to 11. They've heard it hundreds of times and it gets more and more annoying each time.

Studio work can be very frustrating. You're not going to make it any easier by pulling a prima donna act in the middle of the session. If you've never been in a studio before, you might feel like you need to act like a rock star in order to get your money's worth. You will waste money and lose respect.

A studio is not a hotel room. Don't leave empty beer bottles, soda cans, candy wrappers and half-eaten sandwiches laying around. I think part of the reason Screeching Weasel was cut so many breaks by studios over the years was because we always cleaned up after ourselves before we left, and we often took out the trash to boot. In the same vein, just because you're paying a lot of money for studio time that doesn't mean the engineer is your whipping boy. Treat him with respect. "Please" and "Thank you" can make a lot of difference in making your recording session go smoothly.

If you're not needed, take a break. Sometimes your band members will want you around for moral support. If they don't, take a walk. You can go a little stir crazy in the studio and when you start getting squirrelly, you start doing poor work.

Set your budget and stick to it. Most studios will cut you a break if you book large blocks of time. Always book one or two days more than you think you'll need — there may be a power outage or your amp might blow up or the tape machine might decide to stop working. Make sure that you have the studio pencil in the extra time. Don't make them think you're definitely going to spend the extra time — let them know it's just in case you don't finish on time. And try to make sure that your targeted finish date is on a Sunday — that way if you don't use the extra day or two that you booked, they're not valuable weekend days that the studio is losing. If you can buy tape from any source other than the studio, do so. They charge ridiculously high prices for tape and there's no reason to pay that much. Buying your tape from a studio is like driving to an airport concourse restaurant for a burger and fries.

You're not The Eagles. You may run into some difficulties, but you should be able to record and mix an album in five to ten days. If you overanalyze everything you'll drive yourself nuts and make things sound worse through constant tweaking.

Establish control before entering the studio. Allow your band mates to have their say but do not allow them to focus so intensely on their own performances that they waste valuable time. Make sure the buck stops with the band leader when it comes to an objective assessment of a performance or the buck won't ever stop. And if you're the band leader, practice what you preach.

Working for more than a ten-hour stretch is asking for trouble. Working for more than twelve is begging for it. Most engineers will accommodate your goofy marathon sessions but their ears will be so fried and their brains so tired that they'll be essentially useless. So will you.

Don't overproduce. Adding overdubs is terrific. They can turn a great song into an absolute killer. But more often than not, less is more. You don't need four rhythm guitar tracks and you can probably safely can the idea of the chorus of gospel singers without jeopardizing your career.

Have fun but don't forget that this is work. Doing monotonous studio work and making a spontaneous-sounding, energetic album may seem like an impossible combination but as you get used to recording it will become easier.

The last thing I have to say about being in a band is that if you're going to get involved in other aspects of the music scene — promoting shows, publishing or writing for a fanzine, doing a radio show, etc. — make sure you have some outside interests as well. Having immersed myself in the punk scene for too many years, I can tell you that you need breaks. The punk scene is extremely self-contained and if you're the wrong type of personality, like me, it can make dealing with people in the real world more difficult. I haven't worked a real job in ten years. And I don't do a lot of outside work — like producing. I write songs and I write essays and stories. I have to close my office door at night and turn off the ringer on my phone; my office is right next to my living room and sometimes it's difficult to remember what's "work" and what isn't.

As I stated earlier, there are no books or guides for how to live your life as a self-supporting musician. Some people feel that they must always be doing something, so they venture out into other businesses, which is great. But I am not one of those people. I have a short attention span and I have no desire to work on anything about which I'm not passionate. So I write songs, and I write words like these for you to read and I generally stay away from punk events. All of my musician friends, outside of former band members, live in different states. This is good; being too involved in punk scene politics screws up my sense of priority and usually causes me to waste a lot of time doing things I'd rather not be doing, like arguing with people who aren't going to change their minds or mine anyway.

I finally learned to stop reading the majority of reviews of my work. This is extremely difficult. I tried to avoid that stuff for years but it was too tempting. I'm happier now that I don't. Part of the reason it's easier is because I'm not on any fanzine's mailing list any more and I don't buy music magazines. The reviews I read are the ones brought to my attention by others, and those tend to be the type of reviews I want to read. For young musicians, bad reviews can screw you up. You can make unconscious changes to your songwriting or other aspects of your music that you shouldn't (though sometimes you should!). I don't pay attention to the fans any more either. The fans pay the bills but the fans want everything. You can't give everybody everything they want. You have to play your music. If you're successful, with every new release you will lose some fans and gain some. I think this is the way it should be. Fans will always find a reason to complain about you. If you don't act like a good slave, they often fly into a petulant rage (though more often than not it's more of a protracted whine than a rage). You don't need this nonsense. Get away from it. Make sure you stay involved in outside interests. Make sure you stay away from your band members too. Spend too much time with them and you'll end up hating each other — even if you're best friends. You need time away from music and that includes the music scene, your band members and anybody else you deal with professionally. If you don't take this time for yourself, you'll burn out.

I've had to learn most of this stuff the hard way. Almost anything I've told you not to do, I've already done and watched as it blew up in my face. Maybe it's better if we all learn from our mistakes and you'll have plenty of opportunities to do so, but what the hell.

In writing this, I've come to realize that I've probably wasted my time — not that it hasn't been somewhat cathartic. I'm reminded of a surly, drunken Joe King talking a lot of shit behind my back when we brought the Queers on the road with us for their first tour. The details don't really matter; suffice it to say that years later, when Joe had sobered up and was attempting to deal with his own little band of monkeys on the road, he called me up and said in his thick New Hampshire accent, "Ben, I should've listened to you back then. You and John were right. You really gotta have your shit together to do this."

Yeah, well, I told you so.

ALSO AVAILABLE THROUGH **HOPE AND NONTHINGS**

H&N001 : **Incomplete Philosophy Of Hope And Nonthings**
Selected plays by ian pierce
$10.00

H&N002 : **Half Li(v)es**
Anita Loomis / Stories, Poems, and Monologues
$8.00

H&N003 : **Like Hell**
Ben Weasel / A Punk Rock Novel
$12.00

H&N004 : **Devolution**
Sean Benjamin / a play of 40 scenes in random order
$8.00 (release pushed back. Available mid 2002)

H&N005 : **An Apology for the Course and Outcome of Certain Events Delivered by Doctor John Faustus on This His Final Evening** & *The Hunchback Variations*
Mickle Maher / Two One-Act Plays
$10.00

H&N006 : **Weasels In A Box:** *a not so musical journey through partialy truthful situations with eighty percent fictitious dialogue*
John R. Pierson-Jughead-ian pierce / A Punk Rock Novel
$12.00 (release pushed back. write or e-mail for info)

H&N007: **One Hundred and Thirty Neo-Futurist Solo Plays from Too Much Light Makes the Baby Go Blind**
A book of 100 solo plays written and performed by the cast of Too Much Light Makes The Baby Go Blind
(write or e-mail for more info)

H&N008: **Punk Is A Four-Letter Word**
Ben Weasel/Collected Essays from a Punk Rock Journalist. Includes previously unreleased material
$12.00

H&N009: **What the Sea Means: Poems, Stories & Monologues 1987-2002**
Dave Awl/The first book collection of work by writer-performer Dave Awl, poet, Neo-Futurist, founder of The Pansy Kings and surrealist insomniac mystic.
(write or e-mail for more info)

These books can be ordered through mail
Hope And Nonthings
P.O. Box 148010
Chicago, IL 60614-8010
(add 1.50 postage per item. 2.50 Overseas)
Check or Money order made out to:
Hope And Nonthings

www.hopeandnonthings.com (for other puchasing information)